Jane Rubietta brings a sensitivity
bond between Jane and her read
practical, and her message is enc̲o̲u̲r̲a̲g̲i̲n̲g̲. ̲R̲e̲a̲d̲ ̲a̲n̲d̲ ̲b̲e̲ ̲r̲e̲f̲r̲e̲s̲h̲e̲d̲!

—DENNIS E. HENSLEY, author of *Jesus in the 9 to 5*

Finding Your Name is a lovely journey to the miraculous lives found in the Bible. This is a devotional that is also a study in discipleship, yet it carries readers from barren to bounty, telling the stories of Isaac and Jacob in a beautiful, exquisite manner. More than a deeply personal Bible study in devotion, this is also a perfect discipleship tool for small groups.

—KATHI MACIAS, award-winning author of
more than forty books, including *The Singing Quilt*

These are transformational devotionals with great depth. Jane offers a fresh and compelling vision of the lives of Isaac and Jacob, but more than rich words, she has coupled biblical truth with practical ways in which to personally walk from insecurity to inheritance. Especially transformational can be her guide, which leads one to read, contemplate, and act. There is rich and practical depth in these pages.

—JO ANNE LYON, General Superintendent, The Wesleyan Church

Jane Rubietta invites us on a journey from barren to bounty through the lives of Isaac and Jacob that will surprise and inspire you. Packed with Scripture and written with personal witness and wisdom, this ninety-one-day adventure calls us to not only understand, but also live in the promise of full, new life.

—ANDREA SUMMERS, Director of Ministry for Women; The Wesleyan Church

With real-life stories and engaging insight from the Bible, Jane leads readers from insecurity to inheritance to make the lives of Isaac and Jacob real in our lives. What a brilliant connection! Let Jane lead you there—and gain fresh faith and hope for your journey.

—THADDEUS BARNUM, author of *Real Identity* and *Real Love*;
senior pastor of Church of the Apostles, Fairfield, Connecticut

FINDING YOUR NAME

FROM INSECURITY TO INHERITANCE—
THE LIVES OF ISAAC AND JACOB

*To Susan
with love,
Jane Rubietta*

Jane Rubietta

wesleyan
PUBLISHING HOUSE
wphstore.com

Copyright © 2015 by Jane Rubietta
Published by Wesleyan Publishing House
Indianapolis, Indiana 46250
Printed in the United States of America
ISBN: 978-0-89827-898-9
ISBN (e-book): 978-0-89827-899-6

Library of Congress Cataloging-in-Publication Data

Rubietta, Jane.
  Finding your name : from insecurity to inheritance--the lives of Isaac and Jacob
/ Jane Rubietta.
      pages cm
  ISBN 978-0-89827-898-9 (pbk.) -- ISBN 978-0-89827-899-6 (e-book) 1. Bible.
Genesis, XXI-XXXV--Devotional literature. 2. Isaac (Biblical patriarch) 3.
Jacob (Biblical patriarch) I. Title.
  BS1235.54.R828 2015
  222'.110922--dc23

                                2014035269

"The LORD is trustworthy in all he promises
and faithful in all he does."
—PSALM 145:13

To our gracious God who delights to fulfill all those promises.
And to all who wait for their fulfillment.

CONTENTS

For free shepherding resources, visit
www.wphresources.com/findingyourname.

INTRODUCTION

The search for our name and our inheritance began thousands of years ago. We jump into the story with the God who called a man—a man already old by our current standards. God called to Abram and ordered him to leave all his known life and family, and go to a land that God would show him.

Abram, man of faith and adventure that he was, packed up, saddled up, and hauled off, never to return to the land of his initial calling. He chucked everything to throw in his lot with this God who called and wooed him into a life of perpetual traveling and seeking, a life of never quite landing. A life of looking for home.

En route, Abram and his wife, Sarai, encountered miracle and mystery, famine and family issues, war and wonder, and many miles of wandering.

Finding Your Name begins with this nuclear family in a nuclear, as in "self-destructive," season, when their plans didn't seem to match God's timing, or God's plans didn't match their timing. Or perhaps both. Like so many of us, they sometimes took those plans into their own hands. The result was a child, fathered by Abram with the slave woman, Hagar. Sarai orchestrated the plan and then, as often happens with life on planet Earth, especially when we jump the gun on God, difficulties sour the entire era.

After years of barrenness, this couple conceived a child when they were long past childbearing, let alone child-rearing, years. Abram, who became Abraham at this critical juncture, was ninety-nine. Sarai, whose name changed to Sarah, was eighty-nine years old.

God, however, is always able to rescue and bring good from our poor choices. Thankfully, for this family—and for all of us, no matter our family of origin, our own calamitous choices, or our plain old hardships—the inheritance is far greater than the miseries and disasters and flat-out sinful decisions in our lives.

In *Finding Your Name*, we begin with the generations of Hagar, Ishmael, and Isaac, and follow the life of this family clear through to the founding of a fledgling nation, a nation multiplied to include Abraham's thirteen great-grandchildren.

Ninety-two readings, covering Genesis 16–36, take us into the lives of the people during Isaac's lifetime. These readings are intimate reflections on people whose deeper motives, feelings, and thoughts were not directly revealed to us. Some readings take a fictional approach, but in all of them we will try to view our friends in context, both relationally and culturally. We will try to see inside our friends, to understand their actions and reactions, their motivations, their hopes, their wounds. Because, in order to find our true names, to know ourselves as people truly and deeply loved by God, we must, absolutely must, understand our own actions, reactions, and motivations, as well.

These wonderfully human and deeply hopeful people, who helped lay the foundation of our faith, lead the way. May God open the Scriptures to us in new ways, speak to us personally, and lead us into deeper devotion. And may the words of Psalm 68:9 be ours: "You gave abundant showers, O God; you refreshed your weary inheritance."

To prepare to use *Finding Your Name*, it might be helpful to read Genesis 16–36 in one sitting, to catch the sweep of the story, the general direction and plot, and an overview of the characters with whom we will live and journey these next three months.

Four sections complete each deeper devotion: an opening Scripture, a daily reading, a "Traveling Mercy" benediction, and a brief "Note to Self." For the opening Scripture, consider reading a few paragraphs that surround those verses, to gain context, a broader understanding, and application. The daily reading contains multiple opportunities for potential application and is not intended to be gulped down espresso-style. Take time with the questions and truths intrinsic in each reading in order to maximize the application of God's Word. In our world today, we learn much and apply little. This hinders God's unchanging Word from, well, changing us very much. The result, for each of us and for the church at large, is a shallow experience of God's life in us, an experience much less transforming personally, corporately, and globally.

We have inherent in each of us a deep longing to hear God speak over us, personally, as a parent might sing a lullaby over a child. "Traveling Mercy" is a benediction, a "saying well." It shares words that God might say over us. Words of application, healing, love, and hope. This is a place where we press our ear to God's chest, in hopes of hearing God's heartbeat for us.

Finally, "Note to Self." Imagine a sticky note that you post on your mirror or your calendar: Today, don't forget this. Just one thought, a type of application, to carry forward what God's Word offers us.

We find our name as we look to God and God's Word, and begin to become the people God created us to be. People who are changed by the Word of God and transformed for the good of others. People who make a difference in our homes, churches, workplaces, and world.

JUNE DEVOTIONS

THE EVIL EVE

Once Hagar realized she was pregnant, she despised Sarai.

—GENESIS 16:4 NET

Before attempting to explore the interactions between our first families of faith, I struggled with Sarah. Her attitude toward her slave girl, Hagar, really irked me. But through my months of living with these families, Sarah rose from the mystique of legend and my own lack of knowledge, to an imperfect woman I respect. Yes, she left everything behind in Harran. Yes, she experienced great hardship, abandonment, isolation, judgment, dislocation, and disappointment. Yes, she had a hard life. Her husband gave her over not once but twice to two different rulers, refusing to acknowledge their marriage relationship and instead saying they were siblings. Add mishap to misadventure, until the yawning emptiness of her womb led her to desperation.

Sarah cooked up a solution to the embarrassment of family barrenness and her own inability to fulfill the promise God made to them. She sent her slave, Hagar, to bed with Abraham.

This singular machination has been hard for me to forgive. It's ungracious of me, I know.

And then, to deepen the disaster, after all this scheming, when Sarah learned that Hagar was pregnant and her plan had worked, the triangulation in the home accelerated. Eventually, Sarah abused Hagar to such an extent that Hagar ran away into the wilderness. This struck me as small-minded or even cruel on Sarah's part, as an unwillingness to address the widening fault line she'd created in her own marriage and family.

To back up, before fleeing, Hagar "began to despise her mistress" (Gen. 16:4). *Despise* is a complicated word in the Hebrew, but it blends a meaning comparable to "giving the evil eye" with "to curse, blaspheme, revile; to disdain, to be vile." Other shades of meaning exist, but, whichever you take, the word suggests a significant undercutting of her mistress by Hagar.

And Sarah, as the woman in charge of the household and the woman who would continue the legacy God promised, could not allow Hagar's disrespect (a milder word than the original language employs) to remain unchallenged.

Sarah, in spite of her deficits—and who doesn't have them?—was a strong woman. There was nothing codependent about her. She knew how to keep her family in line, and was less concerned about others liking her than she was about fulfilling her role in the promise God made so long ago.

For this, for her years of faithfulness while following Abraham around Canaan and beyond, for her dogged determination to bring God's promises to fruition . . . for all this, and more, I am humbled. True, she seriously mishandled a couple of key decisions. Though lessons abound there, they aren't the only ones that matter. I also recognize that I sometimes act more like Hagar, with my evil eye and disdain on Sarah, than like Sarah herself, who, though imperfect, sought God's promise. What matters more is that God saw fit to include those regrettable events in the Abraham and Sarah story in Scripture. And why does that matter?

Because, in spite of us, God invites us into a promise that far outlives us. And in spite of our backward attempts to fulfill that promise ourselves, God includes us in the family line, just as he did Sarah. God invites people who sin, people who jump ahead, people who plot behind closed doors, people who judge others, people who disdain, people like me—God invites us all into that promise. Into an inheritance that far surpasses any silver or gold, an inheritance that bypasses our spiritual or emotional or physical barrenness and rests on God's provision.

In spite of us, and also, because of us, and through us. And for this, I come alongside Sarah. In the long haul of her life, she feared God, and served God, and cared for her family. She more than lived into the promise God made to her. If I could do the same, I would be most grateful.

TRAVELING MERCY
Dear one,
Imperfect people
Fill my Word
And fill my world.
But remember
I have overcome the world
And have been inviting
Imperfect people
Like you
Into that triumph from the very
Beginning of time.

NOTE TO SELF
Love the imperfects (like me), and everyone else I meet, in
case there are any people besides imperfects out there.

THE AMAZING IMPOSSIBLE

"You will call him Isaac."

—GENESIS 17:19

Eight chapters, Genesis 21–28, detail Isaac's journey from birth to death. Given what we know, Isaac could be considered the timid patriarch. He alone never left the country of Canaan. A well-traveled and faith-talking father and two conniving, wrestling, and impetuous sons bracketed Isaac's life. To say nothing of a wife whose own agenda created a scheme that jeopardized the future direction of the entire family.

If, as behavioral therapists assert, each person makes complete psychological sense, then consider Isaac in the context of his history. Expectations saddled him with enormous responsibility. Forget about the pressure of expanding a tiny family into an entire nation. Forget the pressure of growing up with such a renowned and hospitable (and old) father. Just take his name, for starters. They named him "Laughter." And what a great gift, laughter, a wonderful gift to give others. People live longer if they laugh. Laughter helps heal. It relieves grief and brings delight.

However, anyone who fulfills the role of the clown, the funny person, the make-people-happy child in the family system, knows the pressure of running a constant laugh track.

As much fun as funny people are to have around us—and we all need a few friends who make us laugh—for the laughter, a laughter expectation is tricky. Depression afflicts some noted (and unnoted) comedians, shades of depression that range from bipolar to a generalized sadness.

Laughter offers a way out, and making jokes from hard issues can be good. But it's also work and might hinder necessary healing. The happy-makers might not feel free to pay attention to very real feelings because those aren't great joke fodder. Or they run the risk of noticing the feelings only to mine them for laugh material rather than allowing them to be instructive.

Everyday life is not a happy sack from the fast food emporium, and being named Laughter can force someone into façade-style living: funny on the outside, hollow or bleak or numbed into silence on the inside.

Isaac didn't have the benefit of family systems therapy, but separating ourselves from others' expectations of us becomes critical to personal growth and health. Even more than that, it's essential as we turn our souls toward God, who doesn't expect us to be anyone other than the person we're created to be.

How, then, did Isaac get his name? Sarah laughed in unexpected euphoria, in "I can't believe it! It happened!" delight at his birth. And the year before, when she hid behind the tent flap and heard God announce the coming child, she snorted out a laugh of disbelief (see Gen. 18:12). An eighty-nine-year-old getting pregnant? How funny is that?

And before that, Abraham laughed so hard he fell face-down when God told him, "Your wife Sarah will bear you a son" (Gen. 17:17).

Maybe they named their son Laughter because he was a gift of hope: God converted Sarah's years of disappointment and her painful laugh of disbelief into the reality of a child. A laughter of freedom, for Abraham and Sarah, the fulfillment of years of faith without seeing.

But Sarah and Abraham weren't the only ones waiting on this child. In God's heart, Isaac was beloved, the person through whom the promise would continue. God waited, too, for the right time for Isaac's birth. When Sarah laughed in disbelief, God asked, "Is anything impossible for the Lord?" Turns out, that verb "to be impossible" means "to be amazing, to be surpassing, to be wonderful, to be extraordinary."

The name Isaac, "he who laughs," really came from God. "You will call him Isaac," God said (Gen. 17:19). God laughed with anticipation and joy at the amazing, surpassing, wonderful, extraordinary, impossible birth of this boy.

TRAVELING MERCY
Dear one,
Nothing is impossible for me.
And the impossibles for you
Are really amazing,
Surprising,
Surpassing,
Wonderful,
And extraordinary
Opportunities for me
To love you
And to fulfill
Those impossibles
In your life.
That sets our laughter free—
Rollicking, joyful, rib-tickling
Laughter.
You and me.
The impossible
Has come to be.

NOTE TO SELF
I am, also, the amazing impossible. A miracle.

NO LAUGHING MATTER

But . . . the son whom Hagar the Egyptian had
borne to Abraham was mocking.

—Genesis 21:9

Isaac arrived—the long-awaited promise, the child of the promise, the ultimate gift to a couple too old to consider dreaming such preposterous dreams. God spoke into their version of normal and turned their lives upside down. God called them from obscurity, away from their false gods, away from their past and their present. Called them to live toward a future yet unknown and highly unlikely. Did we mention unusual? And, don't forget that long-ago promise, that still-waiting-for-fulfillment promise: "I will make of you a great nation." After twenty-five years of wondering and watching for that greatness, and a few boneheaded and also disastrous attempts to deliver that promise themselves, Abraham and Sarah learned they were expecting a child.

Sarah was ninety and Abraham a hundred, when Isaac, Laughter, was born.

No doubt everyone had a good laugh, but the first interaction we see with Isaac after his joyful birth is at his weaning party, likely at about three years old. Turns out the only person laughing that day was his half-brother Ishmael, Abraham's first-born son, the child Sarah finagled through the slave girl, thus mangling the household relationships.

This festive occasion for Isaac's surviving the perils of infancy was also an opportunity for Isaac to be confirmed as the heir. No doubt Ishmael felt replaced by this child. He'd enjoyed sixteen years as the apple of his father's eye, and now this clinging and annoying toddler with his invisible crown snared the limelight, the royal robes, and the inheritance. Ishmael likely hadn't been honored with a weaning party, and even if Hagar, his mother, was a legal wife to Abraham, there'd been no real marriage under Sarah's iron-fisted jealousy.

Displacement can do terrible things to anyone, let alone a wounded teenager trying to figure out his place in a complicated family and a complex world. Of course he mocked with laughter the child named Laughter, the king-baby usurping Ishmael's spot in the family. But the laughter ended there, and whatever relationship between Isaac and Ishmael might have developed, it ceased abruptly with Hagar and Ishmael's eviction from Abraham's compound.[1]

Few people escape adolescence without damage, and many of us hurt many people on the journey through. Wounded people wound people, and the best way to stop that cycle is to dress, and maybe address, the wound. What have you believed about yourself, or those around you, or your place in the circle of your family all these years? How much truth crouches in those messages, and how have they impacted you?

Scar tissue is stronger than unwounded skin. The skin's healing process creates a layer of strength and thickness as it binds itself together. So it is with us, emotionally and spiritually: Wounds can help strengthen us if we tend to their proper healing. They can either lead us to more wounds and wounding, or lead us toward strength.

Ishmael and Isaac parted ways at the weaning party, and a celebration of growth sadly ended in a rupture of relationship. We will see them together only one more time in Scripture: their father's burial. The two brothers, together at a funeral. It's too long for a reunion.

If only we could take a page from the book of their lives and come together, instead, in life.

TRAVELING MERCY
Dear one,
I laughed out loud
At your birth, too—
Laughter and mirth
For sheer joy
Of you.
So give that laughter freely.
No inside jokes,
Just share that love,
And nothing will ever
Come between you and me
Or you and others,
As far as you are concerned.

NOTE TO SELF
Love well, and laugh only in joy and kindness.

NOTE

1. Some Jewish interpreters teach that Ishmael lived nearby and frequently visited his father Abraham, and was one of the two servants who accompanied Abraham and Isaac to Moriah, but we have no evidence of this based on the scriptural account.

ISHMAEL'S INHERITANCE

"Do not be so distressed about the boy and your slave woman. . . .
I will make the son of the slave into a nation also."

—GENESIS 21:12–13

Ishmael, at sixteen, was old enough to know what happened. He mocked his half-brother and Sarah caught him, then kicked him out of the party and the family. That was the end of their little respite. Ishmael lost his home, leaving behind any level of comfort, to wander in the desert with his mother, Hagar. On that early morning when they left their tents, he'd hardly been able to look his father in the eyes, and when Abraham put the food and lousy skin of water on Mother's shoulders, he had to turn away from the sight. He thought his heart would shatter, and he couldn't leave quickly enough or get far enough away. Then, when the water dwindled away all too soon, Ishmael crawled into the scrawny shade of a bush to die.

Maybe he thought his father would relent. Abraham loved him; Ishmael knew that. He expected to see him appear any minute, like a mirage in the desert, except for real. But that was not to be. Hope became the mirage, and he closed his eyes against the lie. Tears seeped between his eyelids, and despair eked from him. He might have been sixteen, but he wasn't too old to cry.

An angel found his mother, sobbing nearby, and led them both to a well of water. An entire well! Imagine that. They drank; they lived.

But the angel's words sated his frightened heart more than the water from the well: "God has heard the boy crying as he lies there. Lift the boy up and take him by the hand, for I will make him into a great nation" (Gen. 21:17–18).

Maybe Ishmael's father's inheritance wasn't the only possibility after all. He'd been shut out from all that blessing, one he'd been hearing about for his entire life. But he wasn't shut out from God's blessing and God's protection.

His inheritance would come from God, from his father's God, rather than from the dissolved marriage of Hagar and Abraham.

There is plenty of inheritance to go around; no one holds the sole legacy. Even Isaac didn't—couldn't—monopolize God's generosity. No one can.

You may inherit nothing from your parents' estate. Maybe you have parents who left you with not much more than DNA and disappointment. Or maybe you were well loved but received no financial support as you moved forward with your life. God's legacy is not limited. No one can shut you out from God's blessing. There is plenty to go around.

More than the stars in the sky.

TRAVELING MERCY

Dear one,
There is enough to go around,
And your inheritance
Is vast,
More than water drops in the sea.
Don't shut your heart
To me,
To my longing to bless you.
And don't let another define
That blessing.
My legacy to you
Is unlimited.
So drink
Deeply
From the well
Of lovingkindness
And my deep, endless provision.

NOTE TO SELF

Today, I choose to drink in the truth.

THE WILDERNESS WINNERS

She . . . wandered in the Desert of Beersheba.

—GENESIS 21:14

Wilderness people. You recognize them by the flat look in their eyes, dry as the desert and with a slow lizard blink. Or by the smile that barely moves the skin on their faces and never reaches their eyes. Or they laugh rarely, or laugh too often, as though forcing air through their pipes might force their spirits to join life again.

They are wilderness people. They go through the motions of life, automatons: work, involvements, church, children, spouse, house. Wake up, get up, feed the hungry dependents, start the car, keep moving. Go to bed, to sleep or not to sleep, and then wake up, get up, start the cycle again. They try to mask their gaunt state of soul, the deflation of hope. The puncture wounds from living in barren places make it hard to inhale deeply.

Wilderness people, suffocating from work that squeezes out their gifts and dehydrates their souls. Bloated by too many rejections or too much success. Terrified of losing everything, or terrified they'll never get back what they've already lost to the rigors of wilderness living.

They are Hagar and Ishmael. Sarah grieving her infertility. Abraham without a home. Isaac losing his sight. They are you and I and all the people we know or meet, marred by life's disappointments. They are Esau grieving his blessing and Jacob stealing it. They are Rebekah with her divided family and Lot lost in himself. They are the hungry, the homeless, the wounded, the abandoned. They are children of parents who play favorites. They wait in line at the unemployment office and the soup kitchen and the food pantry and the public aid office. They wait for life to start again.

Wilderness people live in poverty on other continents and on ours. They live in the penthouse downtown and in the mansion nearby. They are you and I. They are our neighbors. Our children. Our relatives. Of course, the wilderness will take anyone and everyone and try to keep them. It's like the opposite of the Statue of Liberty—since no liberty exists in the wilderness—but with the same invitation: send me your poor, your lame, your broken, your brokenhearted, your lost, your grieving. "Send them to me," the wilderness beckons. "All are welcome."

People of the wilderness need shade. They need water in their forsakenness. They need an angel to show them to the well. They—we—need to know that the wilderness is not, in reality, a God-forsaken place. Rather, it's perfect for a rendezvous with God, an ideal place to encounter the God of the wilderness. A place where God hears our tears, understands our fears, and delivers us.

Wilderness people—people like you, like me—need the certainty of the grace available in the wilderness.

We need to know that we can learn to live again, even in a wilderness that never seems to end. Hagar lived. Ishmael became the father of twelve sons. Isaac lived through his wilderness experiences, and his sons lived as well and learned to live fairly well. Perhaps this is why we find such comfort in the stories of Abraham, Isaac, Jacob, and all their family and friends. They qualified for the wilderness, but the wilderness didn't win.

"The people who survive the sword will find favor in the wilderness" (Jer. 31:2). It was true for them. It is true for us. We will survive the sword of life's difficulties. We will find grace in the wilderness. May God open our eyes to see and our hearts to receive.

TRAVELING MERCY
Dear one,
The wilderness cannot win,
Except when it directs you
To me,
To the spring in the desert,
To the life
Found hidden in desperate places.
You can learn
To live
Again,
To laugh
Again,
To love
Again.
And to find life here and now
In the wilderness places
Of your days and nights.
You will find me
When you search for me,
And I will fill your lungs
With my breath.
And you
Will
Live.

NOTE TO SELF
The wilderness works when it leads me to God.

PRAY OR PREY

"Do not be afraid."
—GENESIS 21:17

After Hagar's anger—for of course she was angry about her forced exodus—burned itself out, fear snuck in. Fear, a life-saving and logical emotion in a life-or-death situation. The wilderness is no place for a woman and a teenager, no place to run out of food and water. No place to be without guidance, without a map, without shelter for the night. After living right on the edge of the wilderness, surely Hagar knew the dangers of heat and cold, of hunger, of predators, of losing her bearings.

In the unknown places in all our lives, fear claws at the gate, eager to run rampant, uncaged. It wants to direct the show, to power our adrenaline, to hypercharge our nights and keep us awake. Fear dominates our emotional makeup—and that can't be good.

Fear is a God-given tool. We're born with the capacity for fear, for numerous good reasons, but primarily for survival. Fear is a warning light for our safety and wellbeing, like when the check engine light on the car goes on.

What if, in non-life-threatening situations, when we feel some vague wisp of fear, we stop immediately and ask, "Why? Is this true danger? What is the fear about? Is it reasonable or is it overly dramatic? Is it a childhood reflex that I need to work past?"

Fear occurs for a reason, but even valid responses can magnify our sense of fear. (After all, we decide, fear really was reasonable.) But this magnification can distort and overemphasize those past experiences, since fear that may once have had good reasons for existing may be unwarranted in the present.

When examined, fear becomes our tutor on safety, on emotional health, on physical wellbeing. Fear teaches us to be alert, to assess situations, to take care, and to be on guard. Fear alerts us to danger and can lead us to some creative thinking. And on another level, it teaches us where we are— or aren't—trusting God, and where we are or aren't trusting others. When unchained, fear keeps us from sleep or wakes us in the night, preying upon us.

Fear also numbs us, paralyzing us, as with Hagar who sobbed at a distance from her son while they both waited to die. Terror seems warranted in their dreadful situation, but not passivity. Fear warns us to take care, but it doesn't tell us to lie down and wait to die. To sit at the other end of the field sobbing while someone we love dies of dehydration.

Fear shoots adrenaline through our hearts and then, if we have trained ourselves, inspires our hearts to send out prayers to God. When life doesn't go our way, when we find ourselves exiled and angry, and then frightened, we begin to pray. For wisdom. For clarity. For direction. For the energy to act on those revelations.

Rather than become prey, we can learn to pray in the midst of our fear. Directing ourselves to God, who speaks into the center of the maelstrom, "Do not be afraid." Just then, with those words, God opened Hagar's eyes to see the well of water nearby. Imagine that. Water, in the desert. Lifesaving, life-giving water.

Live and pray. Provision is right around the corner.

TRAVELING MERCY

Dear one,
There is no such thing
As no fear,
But there is wise fear
And unfounded fear.
Perhaps there are resources nearby.
Let me open your eyes to see
And lead you to the well to drink.
Decide today
To live,
To pray,
To live.

NOTE TO SELF

Drink and pray and live.

QUITE A FIX

"God has heard the boy, and knows the fix he's in."
—Genesis 21:17 msg

The good news for every person alive is that God has a plan. Hagar mocked her mistress, but God had a plan. Ishmael made fun of his half-brother Isaac, but God had a plan. In spite of sinful attitudes, in spite of bad behavior, in spite of all the ways we separate ourselves from God, God does not quit on us. God doesn't give up. Doesn't let us sink or swim on our own when we reach out and turn back to him. Doesn't require us to power our own lives on our own steam. Is there a single engine in the world that powers itself? An external source powers every engine I can think of, or it requires an external source to start the internal power.

God has a plan and it is not a DIY project. When he revealed this plan to Hagar, God said, "Lift the boy up and take him by the hand, for I will make him into a great nation" (see Gen. 21:17–21). There are two parts to the plan, one that required Hagar's effort—"Lift him up, take him by the hand." That's where we humans come in. And the other God's power—"I will make a great nation of him."

Maybe that's the rub for you. When you needed someone, no one came into view to assist you. Only a big flashing "Help Wanted" sign in the window of your soul. No one to encourage you, pray for you, hold you, boost you. No one. But that's not quite the truth, not really, not in this world. In spite of all the times when we wanted to post that "Help Wanted" ad more visibly in hopes that someone would come along, lift us, and take us by the hand, we were surrounded by unseen help.

How do you think you got to today? By your own guts and stamina, your own brilliance, your own stunning giftedness? Those helped, maybe. But we have come this far by grace, by divine, unmerited favor or assistance. We don't earn it, don't deserve it, can't make it happen. But God can, and does. It's really part A and part B of the plan, all rolled into one—God satisfying both sides of the instruction to Hagar.

So you think, "Some help this is. Thanks a lot. Look at the mess of my life." Again, we don't see the whole story. We only see our side of the picture, and there's a flip side to every life. The side where God's hand is revealed, where we realize that God has, in fact, been a very present help in times of trouble. God knows the fix we're in.

Sometimes, God shows us a pixel in the picture of our lives, and we realize, in fact, that someone *is* there to take us by the hand and lift us up. And then we get to stand on tiptoe, waiting for the next part of God's word. As God said about Ishmael, "I will make him into a great nation," so God says about us. We are part of the ever-expanding people who love God, and we become people who take others by the hand.

You and me—all part of the plan.

TRAVELING MERCY

Dear one,
The greatness of the plan—
Part A, part B—
Is that it requires
You and me
To make great happen.
I can do it alone,
But how much more
Wonderful
To make great
Together.
I have a plan,
And you are part of it.
So grab a hand
And be part of the crew
Building the great nation
Of heaven.

NOTE TO SELF

Reach out a hand and help two people.

THE GREATEST OF MIRACLES

God was with the boy.

—Genesis 21:20

Ishmael's life might have turned out far differently had he not mocked Isaac, or had his mother been more respectful early on. Of course, with that line of thought we can back up to Adam and Eve. If, for instance, Abraham hadn't been worried about the famine, he'd never have gone to Egypt, and maybe Hagar wouldn't have returned with Sarah to Canaan. If the world hadn't fallen apart morally in Noah's time, Abraham's calling might have changed. If Cain hadn't killed Abel . . . If Eve hadn't seized the fruit . . . The world turns on our actions. A parade of *ifs* marches through our lives daily.

Of course, Ishmael's life might have been different. But dwelling on "if" questions begets only more questions. That was true for Ishmael; it's true for us. Doubts hammer us without mercy if we live in those uncertainties. Life is lived today, not yesterday. So the "I wish I hadn't" and "If only I had" and "What if?" thoughts, while interesting to ponder, place us on a constant roundabout with no exit lanes. It's impossible to move ahead when we're stuck on yesterday's loop.

Ishmael's life on, say, Tuesday, was his life on Tuesday. How it got to be Tuesday and how he handled Monday are history. What Ishmael needed to learn to live in was Tuesday.

Even if the world *does* turn on our actions, and even if yesterday's actions stick a cog in the wheel of our lives and world today—and they do—is God still God?

The miracle is that God's words about Ishmael hold true. "God was with him," the Scriptures tell us. With him. With this man-child who mocked and was run out of house and home, who lost his father and any security he knew. In that place of desolation, Ishmael cried out. God heard, and God was with him as he grew.

Ishmael's reality was much larger than his past mistakes and outright sins. His reality was that God was with him. He didn't deserve God's presence.

But that's also Ishmael's reality: He didn't deserve for God to be with him. It was true for him, and it is true for us. We don't deserve the incredible favor of God being with us. But God lives outside of our expectations and understandings, outside our interpretation of life this side of glory.

God's intentions toward us are for good. That's part of the miracle. We, in our undeserving state, receive God's good intentions. The other part of the miracle, the great miracle, the greatest miracle of all, is that God took the next great step in being with us. God sent Emmanuel—whose name means "God with us."

Whether we live in the Desert of Paran, in the urban desert, or in suburban desolation, the reality is that regardless of the name and size and scope of our desert, regardless of the reason for our desert, God is with us. All day long today, we can look at our wilderness and tell the truth, the greatest reality of all time: "God is with me." We can look back at yesterday and say, "Even so, God is with me." We can gnaw our lip and stare at tomorrow from today's fearful window, and still say with total assurance, "God is with me."

Today, we will live in today, not yesterday and not tomorrow. Today, we live in the truth. Today, we say again and again, as many times as we need to, "God is with me."

TRAVELING MERCY

Dear one,
I am with you,
Whether you see me
Or not.
Stop staring at yesterday,
Except to learn from it.
Stop fretting about tomorrow,
Except to turn tomorrow
Over to me.
I am with you,
And I have tomorrow
Covered.

NOTE TO SELF

Live today, not yesterday.

NO DEAF EARS

"You shall name him Ishmael,
for the Lord has heard of your misery."

—GENESIS 16:11

The name Ishmael comes from a root word meaning "desolate." But that would not be his sole legacy, this young man who never asked to be born and yet was born into a scheming and divided, though promising, household. No, *desolate* would not be his only inheritance, although that word would capture snapshots of his lifetime.

Misery would not be his only moniker, because his name means more than desolate. The sum of the parts of his name means, "God, he heard." Because Hebrew doesn't come with punctuation, Ishmael's name can mean both "God heard Ishmael" and "Ishmael heard God." God named him when he was safe in his mother's womb, though she'd been evicted to the desert and was trying to return to her homeland, Egypt. Hagar, miserable, alone, vulnerable, terrified, yet God said to her, "I've heard your misery." God intervened in Ishmael's life, even then, and told his mother, "I will increase your descendants so much that they will be too numerous to count" (see Gen. 16 for the backstory).

During all those years of growing up, Ishmael could remember this truth, and when he forgot, his mother could remind him: God heard his desolation. God listened to and responded to his heartbreak, his fear, and his loneliness. God heard his longing for his father and for the home of his child-hood. And even though he would never live in those tents again, Ishmael had heard God's reassurance through the angel. Ishmael heard God's words. Over and over he remem-bered them and held them close. "God has heard the boy cry-ing as he lies there. Lift the boy up and take him by the hand, for I will make him into a great nation" (Gen. 21:17–18).

Misery. Desolation. God heard whose misery? God heard Ishmael's mother's misery in Genesis 16, and answered. And then God heard Ishmael's personal desolation, his own des-perate floundering in the desert, and answered. God, he hears.

Sometimes, in our wilderness forays, other people's anguish impacts our lives. We carry their disappointment and grief even as we spend years avoiding our own. Ishmael did not need to carry his mother's misery, tempting and easy as that might have been for him, as it is for any of us. He needed to own only his personal desolation in order for God to hear. And carry it—feel it—we must as well, or we won't recog-nize God's comfort when it draws near or notice God hearing us the way God heard Ishmael.

Misery is not his entire name, nor is it ours.

We have likely cried enough tears in our lifetime, or sup-pressed enough tears, to fill a well of our own. Enough to dehydrate us in our own private deserts. But misery and des-olation are not our inheritance. They are part of living in this broken world, never part of Eden and not part of heaven either.

Our inheritance, like Ishmael's, like Isaac's, is greater than the stars in the sky and sand in the desert. Our inheritance is that God has taken us by the hand—through our parents, maybe. Through the people in our lives, hopefully. Through our adoption into God's very family, so that we are no longer called slaves, the children of the slave woman, desperate and destitute in the desert, but are instead called children of the living God.

Children of the God who hears.

TRAVELING MERCY
Dear one,
Did you think I couldn't hear you?
Hear your tears,
Hear your pain,
Hear you lying there
Beneath the brush?
Did you think I couldn't hear your misery,
Couldn't feel your anguish,
Couldn't remember your name?
No, I remember.
I will never forget.
You are in my will.
You are my inheritance.
You are my very own child,
Child of the living God,
Child of the God who hears.
Can you hear me
Right now?

NOTE TO SELF
Today, do I feel desolate or delighted in?

MULTIPLICATION TABLES

"I will make the son of the slave into a nation also,
because he is your offspring."

—GENESIS 21:13

Talk about amazing grace, how sweet the sound. When Sarah said, "Get rid of that slave woman and her son, for that slave woman's son will never share in the inheritance with my son Isaac," Abraham's heart began a slow shattering. He loved Ishmael, his firstborn son, the son of his own seed. He was greatly distressed, the Scriptures tell us in Genesis 21:11, because it concerned his son.

We've heard very little about Ishmael, other than that Abraham indeed gave him the name as per the angel's instructions during Hagar's first exile (Gen. 16). Which shows that, at least for that moment, Hagar and Abraham talked and he listened to her fantastic story of angelic intervention. But now we listen in on his heart's reaction as Sarah determines this boy's fate, this son of Abraham. His great distress speaks highly of Abraham's integrity and also of his love for this child.

And God's response speaks highly, as well: of God's love for Abraham, and of God's respect for the covenant given to

Abraham more than a quarter of a century before. And of God's compassion for this child, who was, through no fault of his own, part of a messy triangle between three adults.

"Do not be so distressed. . . . I will make the son of the slave into a nation also, because he is your offspring."

This is God, bringing heaven and grace to bear on an otherwise tragic story. This is God, translating love into action for every single child born into this world. For every child born into families that don't function quite right (as in, every family on earth). For every child born of people who didn't plan on babies, or should never have had children, or who cannot be bothered to care for the child. This is for every child born in urban or underserved areas, in outposts in foreign countries, or into poverty and disease and abandonment. For every child ever born, God says, "You, too, are born into this world without being asked. Welcome, child, welcome. I will find you, and call you, and I can bless you. I can make you into a person who influences this world for good. I can multiply your influence beyond your most wide-eyed, far-flung imaginings."

That is how much God loved and honored Abraham.

And that is how much God loves and honors you. This promise holds for you and for me. A child of God, a child of the promise, a child set to inherit all the love the heavens can hold.

TRAVELING MERCY

Dear one,
Do not be distressed.
You didn't ask for this life,
But I am the author of life
And of your life.
You are not an exception
To my love.
You are exceptional,
However,
Because you are mine.
Your life matters,
Your hope matters,
Your longings for safety matter.
You are the child of my own heart,
And I will tend to you.
I will multiply your gifts
In ways that reach to the heavens.
So please,
Do not be distressed, dear one.

NOTE TO SELF

God's words to me determine my journey.
No one else's.

GO AHEAD AND CRY

God heard the boy crying.
—GENESIS 21:17

Imagine Ishmael's confusion, being hurled out into the wilderness by his father, the only person in the entire household he trusted besides his own mother, Hagar. Thrust into the wilderness with a beggar's rations. He was the firstborn son of a wealthy and respected man, and in a flash, all hope and any privilege, real or imagined, vanished. A flash of anger, or jealousy, or both, and Sarah the mistress of the tents wrangled with Abraham until Ishmael and his mother were ousted.

Confusion, yes. Anger, likely. Fear, without doubt. There was Ishmael, this skinny teenager, thrown into the wilderness with only his mother to rely upon for protection and provision, and that pathetic bag of water. Before long, the rations trickled out and fear gushed in. How would they survive in the unfriendly and barren land? How would they live in this terrain, with the desert's breath blowing hot from the west?

Hunger and fear soon won the battle for the boy's soul and demolished the mother's optimism. Hagar shoved Ishmael under a bush to die and then parked herself a long way away.

Her sobs affected him, and finally, in spite of his years of male maturity, he began to cry his heart out.

He would die here. He, who was meant to bring such hope to that waiting and barren household. He, Ishmael, named "God who hears," would die in the desert, destitute and deaf to the purposes of that same God. Heat, hunger, abandonment, and dread all led to an entirely normal response. Ishmael grieved with all the gusto of a teen, broken by disappointment and loss, reined by natural fear.

The Scriptures don't tell us that Ishmael literally wept aloud. They tell us, rather, that God heard Ishmael crying, whether he locked the tears inside or they escaped. We know only that Hagar cried nearby while she expected her son to die. But God knew. God heard the boy's heart. God cared. The one true God sent an angel to direct the bereft mother toward sustenance.

The angel swept in with reassurance and guidance. "Do not be afraid. God has heard the boy crying as he lies there" (Gen. 21:17–18). Tears are never wasted, not real tears. Those tears got God's attention. Those tears turned the key in the lock of Ishmael's future, and sprang open the door of God's provision.

Tears and fear are natural reactions for all of us. That God heard Ishmael weeping encourages us to feel both the fear and the tears, and to trust that the God who hears will, indeed, hear our hearts and answer. So go ahead and cry. There's plenty of pain to release, and plenty of God's comfort to go around.

TRAVELING MERCY

Dear one,
Tears are good.
Cry them
Loud.
Cry them
Real.
Direct them to me.
Because I hear
Your loss,
Your pain,
Your destitution,
Your fear,
Your heart.
So cry.
And then
Listen to me,
Because
I am the God
Who heals—and leads—
The brokenhearted.

NOTE TO SELF

Tears lead me to God's sustenance.

LISTEN AND LIVE

"Do not be afraid. God has heard."

—Genesis 21:17

Her second shot at the wilderness, Hagar quickly ran out of resources, including the determination to survive. Had that been snuffed out of her, perhaps because as a slave she'd been taught to ignore any internal emotional rumblings? She surely got that message when, pregnant with Abraham's child, she challenged Sarah's authority, and Sarah promptly pitched her out the door. On her return, with a child incubating in her womb, she knew she needed to button her lip and mind her manners at least in the presence of Abraham's first wife, ignoring her emotions or out she would go again. When Ishmael's attitude earned them refugee status, no surprise that her will to survive seemed to disappear.

Perhaps that's the message you've received throughout your life. "If you know what's good for you, you will . . ." or "you won't . . ." For many people, survival instincts subside into passivity, smothered by others in authority who do all the thinking and feeling. Better to be seen and not heard, don't make waves, keep your voice down and your gaze to the ground. Unless they keep thinking and growing, these children end up as adults who are seen but not heard. Not heard by anyone else or sometimes by themselves, unable to recognize the state of their own soul.

Hagar collapsed into tears in the wilderness, her fear of death winning over her desire to survive. But those tears leaked past the threshold of fear and caught God's attention. God spoke through an angel, "Do not be afraid."

The angel wasn't saying, "Don't ever be afraid." No, fear is a God-given survival tool. Rather, the angel was saying, "Don't let fear run your life and ruin your life. Listen to the fear and bring your fear here."

Don't be afraid? Easy to say, hard to do. Until the next words, because God would deliver: "Take the child by the hand . . ." And behold, water. Lifesaving water, a well full of water, an endless supply of water in the wilderness.

Hagar was a victim, but because of the angel's intervention, she became a victor. Her child lived and became the father of twelve sons. Hagar became the grandmother and great-great-grandmother of many people. Hagar the matriarch. Who would have predicted that back in Egypt? Or even in the tents of Sarah and Abraham?

Ultimately, Hagar listened to her soul and to the God of the wilderness, and lived. Fear did not win.

God won.

TRAVELING MERCY

Dear one,
Just as I asked Hagar,
So I ask you,
"What is the matter?"
Listen to your heart,
Listen to your soul,
Listen to the situation,
But listen, too, to me.
For I have called you,
And the wilderness
Is no surprise to me.
Fear can save your life
Or own your life.
So bring it to me,
Listen to me,
And live.

NOTE TO SELF

Hear the fear; take it to God.

REFUGE FOR A REFUGEE

She went on her way and wandered in the Desert.
—GENESIS 21:14

Hagar and Ishmael's exile from Abraham's home marked a turning point for the tiny family. The refugees wandered in the wilderness until draining their scant resources, and then Hagar laid her son under a bush to die. But God met her in her exile.

Maybe you're the one in exile. Maybe you've been abandoned by the people who are supposed to love you and you've cried yourself dry in the wilderness. Maybe you're fleeing for your life (or wish you could flee) and you've ended up parched in the desert through no fault of your own.

This was Cassandra's story. Married to a violent man, she endured a decade of being battered and bruised, her bones broken and eyes blackened. But throughout the marriage, Cassie refused to hate, refused to return evil for evil, refused to become bitter. She held on to God.

And one day, her husband dove at her with a knife, chasing her around their home. His slashes and poundings left gashes and holes in the walls, and upturned furniture. Blood flowed.

Fighting for her life, Cassie wrested the knife from his grip. In seconds he was dead, and she was barely alive.

She changed from her bloodstained clothes to an orange jumpsuit. The police threw her in jail for murder.

But Cassie's God took her hand and turned her cell into a refuge. God converted the wilderness into an oasis, and she at last was safe and could heal. In those months of recovery, women noticed—inmates whose lives were equally difficult and dreadfully painful, whose crimes even more horrific. But they saw in her peace, an other-worldly light in response to incarceration. Cassie's cell glowed with God's presence as she buried her face in the Scriptures and prayed. Her bitterness dissipated, and her heart expanded with an unquenchable love.

Before she won her freedom, Cassie led countless others to theirs—freedom in Christ, freedom in forgiveness, freedom in being loved for the first time without strings.

And so her wilderness became a refuge and place of healing for herself and many. God put her near a well and she drank deeply, then invited others to quench their thirst on the living water freely offered.

Whatever the circumstances, it's not too late for God to convert your refugee status into a refuge, into freedom and healing. God's words to you, to us all, are the same as God's words to Hagar and Ishmael: "I have heard your crying."

God waits, listens, for our heart. So cry. And then invite God, invoke God, to convert those tears to water in the desert.

TRAVELING MERCY

Dear one,
I hear your tears.
I hear your heart.
I know you are broken
And feel abandoned.
But you are not abandoned.
You are never alone.
I am here,
And I am
Water for your thirst
And balm for your wounds.
Your wilderness will be
A conversion point,
A place of healing
For you and many.
Come to me.
Trust me.
Let me open your eyes.
There's water close by.

NOTE TO SELF

God is my refuge and my strength.

WILDERNESS GIFTS

He lived in the desert and became an archer.

—GENESIS 21:20

Ishmael didn't settle for just getting older in the desert. Growing up chronologically wasn't the only way he could grow. Even his story is told from the viewpoint of an archer: Hagar sat a "bowshot" away from where Ishmael lay under that bush. Who but an archer would call it a bowshot?

To survive the wilderness, Ishmael needed to find food. He would need to enroll in the Hunter and Gatherer School of Survival and fast. We don't know how he spent his childhood, whether he used a painted target with red concentric circles to hone his skills, threw rocks to practice his aim, and worked his core to develop stability. Archery as a hobby likely wasn't included in his daily agenda. While it's possible he hunted food for Abraham's family, we have no idea how his past actually prepared him for his present and provided him a way into his future. But circumstances forced him to perfect his bow and arrow skills in short order.

The desert is good for that. It forces our hand: Will we live well here, or give up here? Regardless of how unexpected or expected our deserts might be, we get to choose; we continue to exercise options, even if they're negative ones. Ishmael, however bad his rap prior to this, made the most of the wilderness. He didn't prefer the wilderness, surely. It would have been easier in many ways, perhaps, to be in Abraham's tents.

Ishmael did not sit around bemoaning his past or moaning about his present. Hunger and fear serve as motivational power tools. After God promised to be with him, he got up and got going. Life in the wilderness? So be it. Learn to hunt. Don't know how? Position arrow. Pull back string. Let it go. Do it again until you hit a target. Load, pull, release. Repeat until you hit something edible. Repeat until you kill it.

When we find ourselves in difficult places, unexpectedly hard spots, we get to choose. Sit under a bush and die? Or get up and learn to hunt?

We can prepare for the wilderness times of our lives by honing our focus and sharpening the arrows of our wits. Sometimes we can avoid the wilderness by wise choices and living with integrity. But ultimately, the wilderness is an unavoidable stop on this tour of duty called life. It will demand everything of us and offer little in return. But we don't need to crawl under a bush.

Unemployed? Sharpen your arrows by taking a night class or volunteering while you keep applying for jobs and praying your voice hoarse. Feeling empty in this hard place? Sign up for an intensive Bible study class at your church or a nearby church. Not sure about this God stuff? Join a prayer group and see what happens.

When we find ourselves in the desert, thirsty and afraid, we can sharpen our arrows and practice our aim. We can pen our own wilderness chapters. The Enemy won't win here. God wins. We know how the story ends.

TRAVELING MERCY

Dear one,
This is partly
A choose-your-own-ending story,
Though in some places
You didn't choose.
Now you get to choose
To sharpen your arrows.
To die here
Or grow here:
What will it be?

NOTE TO SELF

Sharpen arrows. Check.

TOO SOON TO QUIT

God was on the boy's side.

—GENESIS 21:20 MSG

Kids think their parents should know how to fix absolutely any problem, and surely Ishmael felt no differently about his mother, Hagar. She'd traveled the world—well, from Egypt to Canaan, which was like traveling the world as far as her son was concerned.

When his father told them good-bye, Ishmael didn't know what to think. He could hardly blame himself for their exile—or could he? Should he?

But their exodus from the tents of Abraham and Sarah, their sojourn in the wilderness, would be bearable because he trusted his mother. She'd been his staunch defender all his days, as much as was possible as slaves in another's home. So when he couldn't eat because he needed water to digest the food, in spite of his big teenager attitude, he broke down. He looked to his mother. She could fix this problem.

Except she couldn't. When she pushed him under that bush and stumbled away, bawling, he felt more helpless than ever in his entire life. He couldn't save his mother, and it would appear that his mother couldn't save him. So he resigned himself to wait. For what, he was pretty sure he didn't want to know. When Hagar walked so far away he couldn't even hear her cry, something in him began to die.

He was alone. Absolutely abandoned. By his mother. By his father. By Mistress Sarah. And God's words to his mother, so long ago, when she carried him tucked safely inside her womb? "You shall name him Ishmael, for the LORD has heard of your misery" (Gen. 16:11). She'd told him that story all his life, so what was he doing beneath this bush? He wanted to laugh, but that required energy. (Besides, the last time he laughed that mocking laugh, he ended up here.) So much for the Lord, so much for being heard, so much for angels who show up in your desperate times and rescue you with a fresh word from heaven.

And isn't that the way we feel, as well? Deserted, abandoned, expecting help that never seems to come? We don't see the angel, heaven seems silent, and our hearts shrivel like ancient fruit.

It's too soon to give up, friend. It's too soon to stop breathing and stop hoping and stop watching for that angel. Because God hasn't given up, even though wilderness hallucination makes us believe we are orphaned in the barrens. That is a patent untruth, and if we give up now, we will not know that on the other side of that bush is a well of fresh water.

So keep watch. And don't quit.

TRAVELING MERCY

Dear one,
In your exhaustion and in your thirst
You want to quit.
In your abandonment,
In your loneliness,
In your despair,
You want to quit.
But hold on.
Help is on the way.
Just as I was with Ishmael,
I am also with you.
Because I am
The I Am—
Not the "I might"
Or the "I could if I feel like it"
Or "I am if you are polite."
I Am.
I always am.
And I am here now.
So lift up your eyes;
Help is coming.

NOTE TO SELF

I am not abandoned.
I will watch for help.

BEHOLD THE LAMB

"God himself will provide the lamb for the burnt offering, my son."

—GENESIS 22:8

Many years after Ishmael and Hagar's exile, Abraham awakened his son, Isaac, for their dawn trip. The mood was sober as Abraham chopped wood, and Isaac pondered the mysterious agenda there in the last-minute dark of night. The servants, too, stood by, and every heart pounded in the same odd beating of inexplicable fear.

Isaac's mother. Where was she? He turned to look, but the door of her tent flapped empty. The sojourn began, the travel to the unknown destination slowed by his aged father's steps. He was still a mighty man—he'd chopped the wood himself, hadn't he?—but no match for Isaac, in the strength of young manhood. Still, the wood cut into Isaac's shoulders and even deeper into his soul as they walked, Isaac adjusting his steps to his father's stride.

Scripture records only one conversation between them on this muted journey to Moriah. The servants waited at the base of the mountain, and Isaac and his father climbed forward together.

"Father?" Isaac asked.

"Yes, my son?"

"The fire and the wood are here, but where is the lamb for the burnt offering?"

"God himself will provide the lamb for the burnt offering, my son."

And on they climbed, father and son, trekking to an unknown ending.

At the place God told him about, Abraham built an altar and carefully laid the rocks and then the bundled wood. When he turned to his son, Isaac looked for the sacrificial lamb.

Eyes glinting with unshed tears, his father's hands gripped Isaac's arms. Then the young man fully realized his father's intent: Isaac would be the sacrifice.

Everything Isaac knew about his life flashed before him: the long-awaited child, named by God, by *God*, "He who laughs." He was loved, treasured. The one through whom the promise would continue.

So why this, why the altar, why him?

Just as God asked Abraham to break with his future—*lekh lekha*, in Genesis 22:2—so God asked Isaac, nonverbally, to break his ties with the future. To entrust himself to God, entirely confident in God's love and goodness and provision for him.

And Isaac climbed on the altar, willing to give everything to the God who promised everything. His father tightened the bindings and swallowed hard, the tears streaking his face and running into his beard. "My beloved son, I'm so pleased with you," he must have thought as love flooded his bloodstream. And then he raised the knife.

The touch of the blade made Isaac's skin tingle. Then that voice from heaven. "Abraham. Abraham!"

The angel called him twice, urgent in mission.

Isaac had never heard this voice before—at least, never so clearly as this. For the first time, when he gave himself entirely up to God, he heard heaven's voice. Calling his father by name. And his father's answer, arm upraised, tears in his eyes: "Here I am."

"Do not lay a hand on the boy," the voice said. "Do not do anything to him. Now I know you fear God, because you have not withheld from me your son, your only son."

Isaac's entire body pressed with relief into the wood and tinder beneath him. God had saved him. God spoke, Abraham answered, God saved him. Whether the voice was God's, Christ's, or an angel's has been long debated. What we know for sure is that the voice came from heaven, and that Isaac experienced God's deliverance.

Abraham did not withhold his son from the God he loved. And Isaac did not withhold himself from his father or his God. That day, truly, Abraham's God became Isaac's God. "The Fear of Isaac," his own son Jacob would call God decades later (Gen. 31:42).

The ram in the thicket rattled the bushes and became the substitutionary sacrifice, and after many years, the lamb, the "Lamb of God, who takes away the sin of the world" (John 1:29), would offer himself as a living sacrifice.

For this day, on Mt. Moriah, heaven met earth, a foreshadowing of the day when heaven would meet earth once again, and earth would meet heaven, through Jesus Christ, the only begotten Son of God. God's firstborn Son, the son of Abraham, Isaac, and Jacob.

TRAVELING MERCY

Dear one,
My plans are larger than you can see,
Larger than the sea
And all the grains of sand.
Offer yourself wholly
To me
And see.
Break with your hopes for the future—
For am I not your future?
Will I not care for you?—
And offer yourself to me.
And then see
What I will do.
I have already provided
The Lamb for the offering.

NOTE TO SELF

What do I withhold from God?

AN ALTAR OF THE HEART

Therefore, I urge you . . . in view of God's mercy, to offer
your bodies as a living sacrifice, holy and pleasing to
God—this is your true and proper worship.

—Romans 12:1

Isaac. Willing to walk beside his father three days to the mountain, willing, during those many footsteps, to consider his options. With monument-sized faith, he pressed forward, surely his soul whispering the truth to him after he asked his father the only recorded question of the journey, "Where is the sacrifice?"

Isaac realized his father's intent—Isaac himself would be the sacrifice. And in that moment, he made a stunning decision. He was not powerless. He could have shouldered his father aside and walked away. Instead, he willingly lay down on that pyre, willingly accepted the bindings that lashed him to the wood his father had chopped three days earlier.

He chose to present himself as a sacrifice. To offer himself up to God, to lay his heart and soul and hopes and dreams on that altar, to release absolutely everything to the God of his father Abraham.

To his God.

Many years later, Paul would write, in Romans 12:1, "Therefore, I urge you . . . in view of God's mercy, to offer your bodies as a living sacrifice, holy and pleasing to God—this is your true and proper worship." All of us, alive and wriggling, but still offering ourselves in entirety, to God.

Unlike Isaac, I present only parts of myself to God as an offering, parts of my life and only certain relationships. But the rest of my life, I operate by myself, I keep to myself, for myself. Paul told us to give it all, and perhaps, even, when we hear Jesus' words, "Love the Lord your God with all your heart and with all your soul and with all your your mind and with all your strength" (Mark 12:30), we flash back to Isaac, who offered all of himself, totally. All his heart, soul, mind, and strength. Had he not chosen to give God his entire self, he couldn't have stayed on the altar and would never have followed through with the sacrifice.

Isaac was a willing, living sacrifice. He was not there under duress, under fear of what his father would think of him if he sat up, swung his legs over the side, and walked away. He lay there because, in the deepest wrestling of his soul, he wanted to give himself to God. The binding represents that certainty that he would not flinch away at the final moment of offering.

Today, I have so few true sacrifices to offer God. Very little money. A few paltry gifts.

So few means of giving myself entirely to God. Even when I pray, I am often concerned with my agenda. My distractible brain leaps about like a flea on a sheep's coat, and soon there is nothing sacrificial whatsoever about giving even my attention to God, let alone my life.

To die to myself—to lay myself on the altar, willingly, as Isaac did—is to offer all of myself to God. My motives, wishes, dreams, problems, and the tiny control issues I have that surface only every few . . . seconds. To die to myself is to say, "I want nothing more than God. *Nothing* more than God. And nothing less than God."

This is not my standard approach to daily life and faith. I'm embarrassed to say how infrequently moments (seconds) of total abandonment to God occur in my life. But perhaps the key to a living offering, is just that: living. It is living sacrificially this moment, for life can only be lived, can only be offered, one moment at a time.

And so, for this moment, I can say, "I am wholly yours, O Lord. Here I am."

Then, when I lace up my running shoes and begin to race off, I can offer myself again.

And again.

And then, to invite God: "Lord, bind me tightly to your heart, let my heart be your altar. Bind me with cords of love so that I never want to leave."

TRAVELING MERCY
Dear one,
Just this moment.
A lifelong commitment
Lives itself
One moment at a time.
Let's start now.
Offer me your heart.
You already have my love.

NOTE TO SELF
Love, one second at a time.

THE COURAGE TO STAY

It is through Isaac that your offspring will be reckoned.

—GENESIS 21:12

Call him passive if you want—and some commentators do, since he experienced far fewer adventures than his father or his sons did—but Isaac was courageous to follow God. How could Isaac, after all, explain this God who ordered Abraham to kill him—to strap him to a pile of kindling, slash his throat, then burn him as an offering?

Surely that left some emotional scars. Whether he was fourteen or twenty-four, or even thirty-seven as some Jewish commentators suggest, what happened inside his psyche in terms of his relationship with his father?

Did Isaac, every single day for the rest of his 180 years, replay that early morning journey toward Moriah? Did he hear his father's labored breathing as they trudged together for three long days, with Abraham leaning on his strong son and Isaac trusting his father? *Trusting*. Forever after, did the scent of the wilderness at sunrise constantly toggle Isaac's mind to that dreadful dawn? Did he sometimes jolt awake with his heart thudding in a panicked arrhythmia, his thoughts flapping about like birds startled by a predator? Every day, for the rest of his life, did Isaac live with the certainty that he'd been saved? Rescued from death, from unspeakable death on a crude altar with a knife to the throat—a knife held in the hands of his aged and beloved father.

Then did relief deluge his system and swat down the panic whenever he remembered that an angel had intervened and stopped his father's hand? Did he recall, after the flash flood of fear coursed in his veins, that a ram had appeared nearby at the precise moment of necessity?

Or, instead, did the memory of miraculous deliverance dull, like even the most miraculous deliverances do? And did the pain of his father's actions sharpen itself daily on the rasp of anger and bitterness and abandonment?

He could have rejected faith and walked away from God after that long trek to the altar. He could have sworn off God as a whole lot of hooey and never looked back. We all know people who've run from the God they don't understand, rather than staying around for the God they do understand or trying to follow God by faith. Maybe we've even had our moments or seasons of running.

The altar was Isaac's defining moment. We see Isaac's courage in that he stayed: he stayed in relationship with his father and with his father's God. More than that, his father's God became his God. And because of his courage and God's faithfulness, the promise God made in Genesis 17:19, before Isaac's birth, began to bear fruit: "I will establish my covenant with him as an everlasting covenant for his descendants after him."

The altar is our decision point, our defining moment, as well. Here we can pivot on our heels and walk away, because we don't understand this world or God's hand in the events of this world. Or we can stay put and choose to trust. Because Isaac stayed, we can say with Paul, "Now you, brothers and sisters, like Isaac, are children of promise" (Gal. 4:28).

And that's a definite.

TRAVELING MERCY
Dear one,
Faith makes no sense
In a world of broken promises.
Lash out at me,
But don't lash yourself to the altar
Of misunderstanding
Or hatred
Or vengeance
Or isolation.
Don't bind yourself with another's
Misunderstood actions
And then separate yourself
From me.
Your experiences are vital,
But see them
Through my eyes.
Stay with me.
You will see,
Sooner
Or later.
I promise.

NOTE TO SELF
I will not run away in spite of doubt.

NOT UNDERSTANDING
DOES NOT EQUAL NOT BELIEVING

Though you have not seen him, you love him;
and even though you do not see him now, you believe in him
and are filled with an inexpressible and glorious joy.

—1 PETER 1:8

Wouldn't it be easier to gloss over some of the difficult passages in the Scriptures, passages that depict God in a less-than-glowing, loving, and beneficent way? Or to leave God and the Bible alone, entirely? After all, what kind of God sends a flood and wipes out all of creation, handpicking one little family to save, as in Noah's experience? What kind of God promises a massive inheritance of people more numerous than the stars, and blessings upon blessings, and then toys with the couple through years of infertility? And then tops it off by waking up the happy father and ordering him to kill that son?

I don't have a wise and scholarly answer for these questions (nor have the theologians I have read answered them particularly well). And I don't have responses to the many other questions like them that concern God's behavior, our interpretation of it, or both. God lives outside of us and our finite time. God sees the beginning from the end. God's promises and presence trump the problems I wrestle with in the Scriptures. Maybe this is simplistic.

But ultimately, faith is, well, faith. Why would I expect to understand God? God is God, and I am, thankfully, not. The very fact of God defies my understanding except in a very pre-school manner of spirituality and theology. But should I refuse to throw in my lot with God simply because I can't explain God?

Even though I don't understand the part of God that tells Abraham to sacrifice his son, what I do understand about God is that, at the moment of proof, God halted the knife. God halted the sacrifice and provided a ram in the thicket.

There I see the essence of God. The God who provides a substitute. The God who saves the child and the father. The God who would, eventually, send the ultimate substitute in the form of the Lamb of God.

Call me simple. But even when I don't understand the sacrifice—can't grasp that it reflects, centuries down the road, that God would send Christ to the cross—still at a very basic level the rescue of Isaac speaks to me of love.

That God, that God of love, I can trust with my life.

TRAVELING MERCY
Dear one,
Faith doesn't have all the answers,
But rather believes,
Even when not seeing,
Even when not knowing.
Know this, though:
That I have loved you since forever,
And everything in your life
And in this world
Is intended to draw you to me.
So don't let your doubts shove you away,
But rather bring them to me.
One day you will see.

NOTE TO SELF
I choose to believe, even when I don't understand.

NOTHING TOO BIG . . . OR SMALL

"The LORD, the God of heaven and the God of earth."

—GENESIS 24:3

To the end of his life, Isaac's father looked to the Lord, his God. God had provided him with a son, Isaac, and then saved him from certain death on the altar. Now it was time for a bride for Isaac, and after half a lifetime of trusting God, Abraham changed nothing about his approach.

Forty and single, the sole heir to the promise, Isaac needed a bride. He needed children. He'd mourned for his mother long enough. Too feeble to make the trek himself, Abraham chose his most trusted servant to play matchmaker for Isaac. So important is this matchup to the ongoing fulfillment of God's promise, this vital journey takes an entire chapter, all sixty-six verses, to relate.

Abraham commanded his chief servant, held in Jewish tradition to be Eliezer, the same servant he tried to make his heir after so many years of infertility. "Go to my country and my own relatives and get a wife for my son Isaac" (24:4).

Abraham didn't just order his servant. He ordered his own understanding and reminded himself and his servant of the core truth, the bedrock of their existence, the hope and the reason for their vagabond lifestyle. "Promise me," he said. And then he put forth the foundation of his faith: "The LORD, the God of heaven and the God of earth."

What a comfort to remember, in a season of uncertainty, of searching, that our God is the God of heaven *and* the God of earth. The God of heaven—the God who rules the heavens, who commandeers the stars and set the planets in motion, who lights the day with the sun and the night with the moon. The God of heaven—who rides the wings of the wind. The God who harnesses clouds for chariots. The God who anchors us to the earth with gravity. This God.

This God, the God of heaven, is also the God of the earth. All things of earth, God oversees, God understands, God knows. This is the God, who said at the pinnacle of creation, "It is not good for the man to be alone" (Gen. 2:18). How reassuring, as Abraham prayed for a bride for his son Isaac, to know that the God of the earth would care about such details, to the point of initiating the solution. The God of the earth—the God who is not diminished by the immensity of the earth and the depths of its canyons, who spoke and created all things—this God cared about Isaac's bride. This God who knows where the wind originates. This God who calls forth rain and waters the earth. This God who calls people from nowhere and leads them into a promise larger and grander than anything imaginable. This God who promised nations descending from an old woman and an even older man, and gave them a son. And this God cared about the details of that son's life: like, where to find a bride who will bear children and continue the heritage promised to Abraham and his family line.

Today, as I consider all the knots and tangles in the cord of my life, Abraham's truth comforts me. The God of heaven and the God of earth hears our deepest needs and greatest longings. Nothing is too earthy or too grand for this God.

This God. The God of heaven and earth. Abraham's God, my God, your God.

TRAVELING MERCY
Dear one,
I still am I AM.
I am still
The God of heaven and
The God of earth.
So tell me what you need,
What you hope for,
What you wait for.
Nothing is too big,
Nothing is too small
For me
To care about
For you.

NOTE TO SELF
Here's my list, God: _____.
(Fill in some blanks.)

TAILOR-MADE ANSWERS

Before he had finished praying . . .

—GENESIS 24:15

The servant loaded the caravan with gifts and made his painstaking way to Harran. Upon arriving, he left nothing to chance. He spelled out his entire list of requests, and the specific ways God should be clear about the answers: The woman who offered him a drink of water and who offered to water his camels also would be the wife God had chosen for Isaac. He prayed with one eye open to watch for results, and before the words entirely left his mouth, a woman appeared on the scene.

Don't we, too, pray with one eye open? The journey is long and our throats are parched with thirst. We've itemized our list, and now the legs of our faith ache with the weariness of seemingly fruitless travel. Unlike in the servant's case, in our life, no one appears by the stream to offer us a jug full of water and no one offers to water our camels or even our potted plants while we're gone. Nothing happens. We feel left out, unchosen, like maybe God answers everyone except us. All those passages about seek, knock, ask—we've done all that but hear nothing. No answers, not a yes or a no. Nothing.

How easy to feel like we're on the outside, way outside the winner's circle of people who pray and get answers, brothers and sisters who ask for signs and receive confirmations as clear as a text from heaven. Like Abraham's servant, whose answers arrived before he said amen. Maybe they are godlier than we are, we think, since we have so many dropped calls to God. This walk by faith is more like a blind stumble sometimes, more scraped knees and bruised shins than garlands of roses around our necks.

Coveting another's journey, or answers to prayer for that matter, is still coveting. Whether we're comparing family trees, cars in the garage, or the daily grind of work, we come awfully close to the boundary of coveting. Of course another's blessings seem better than ours—it's all about perspective.

But it's also about packaging. God knows exactly the right combination of blessings for our particular journey. God knows precisely how and when to respond to our urgent pleadings for answers from heaven. God knows what we need and knows what kind of blessings fit us best. Besides, to covet the way God works in others' lives means we also have to consider their whole package: We see only the outside, the sometimes glossy, airbrushed travel magazine cover of other people's journeys. Much as we might like to try on their blessings for size, we don't want to don their pain.

God knows we sometimes think we'd love to trade. But God also knows us, knows our needs, and knows exactly how to care for us. One thing about Abraham's servant: He asked for signs to give him wisdom, but trusted God to choose what was best, what kind of woman was best, for Isaac's life.

God's love—and God's answers—in our lives are tailor-made for us. We can learn to wear our own life well, trusting God's unique choices for us. And rather than long for another's closet, we can recognize, and wear, our own life with confidence.

TRAVELING MERCY
Dear one,
Go ahead;
Ask me.
You do not have because
You do not ask.
So please ask.
But know, too,
That I know you.
And I know what fits you
And the people you love.
So ask,
And when you ask,
Trust,
And when you trust,
Wait.
Wait for me
To show you how I'll love you.
My blessings will fit you
Perfectly.
Wait and see.

NOTE TO SELF
God's work in my life fits me perfectly.
I just need a better mirror.

UNIQUE JOB QUALIFICATIONS

She . . . quickly lowered the jar to her hands and gave him a drink.

—Genesis 24:18

News traveled slowly or not that far or even not at all in those days. Hospitality, so critical to a traveler's survival in the Middle East, also provided a natural conduit for information along the route. Perhaps it's not surprising that Rebekah rushed to greet the man who appeared near the watering spot toward the end of the day — she might learn exciting news of the hinterlands, lands a typical girl in that era might never see. Perhaps it's not unusual that she would offer to water his numerous camels, though each camel might have needed as many as twenty-five gallons of water — which meant a lot of trips to refill the jug Rebekah hefted onto her shoulder.

Of course, these particular camels carried loads of gifts, and camels indicated a degree of wealth beyond an everyday scraping-by existence. Maybe she saw those gifts and those camels, assessed the situation as one that might be profitable for her, and rushed into hospitality.

The Scriptures don't tell us about her motives. But we see her generous nature, her willingness to expend herself for a stranger, and her compassionate understanding of the need for water after a long day's travel.

Uncomplicated hospitality doesn't come easily for everyone. No questions asked, come right in, let us feed and house you even though we don't know you and you've appeared out of nowhere. You might have a history, you might be dangerous, or might be contagious. In our day, and in many countries, hospitality of this magnitude packs some legitimate risk. Besides that, we'd have to stop what we are doing, all the important tasks and agendas that occupy our attention. Tasks like drawing water for the family. Like finishing up the chores for the day so we can put up our feet in front of the movies-on-demand and suck down an icy beverage straight from the fridge.

Rebekah challenges us. With no idea that the man before her was her great-uncle's servant and that a divine opportunity waited for her, she recognized a need that she was qualified to meet. She saw an opportunity to serve, even if at great effort, and by lowering the jug, she stepped into the middle of God's plans for her future.

Hospitality, whether or not it's one of our particular gifts, is still our calling. Maybe it's eye contact and a smile for someone on the train or a word of encouragement to the exhausted mother in the grocery store whose screaming children teem over the sides of the cart. Perhaps it's the gift of asking another about her life, her week, or her hopes that day. Or the hospitality of listening for someone's pain.

Maybe Jesus referred to this simple practice, so many years later, when he said, "If anyone gives a cup of cold water . . ."

(Matt. 10:42). There is a need we are uniquely qualified to meet. Today, we lower our jug. And even if it's not a man and his camels standing on our stoop, we offer water.

TRAVELING MERCY
Dear one,
Of course you are thirsty.
This is why I've invited you
Over and over
To come to me.
All who are thirsty.
So come.
And then,
When someone asks you for a drink,
You can lower your jug
Because you have been filled
To the brim
With my love,
A river
That never, ever
Ends.

NOTE TO SELF
Fill up and then pour out.
There's more water in the river.

THE ESSENCE OF FAITH

[He] bowed down and worshiped the LORD.

—GENESIS 24:26

When the servant recognized God's astounding, to-the-letter answer to his prayers for leading, he "bowed down and worshiped the LORD." He bent double, in full view near the watering spot, in front of all those young ladies, and worshiped. All those days on the road, exhausted, grimy, thirsty. He prayed and God answered, and then the servant answered God's answer with worship. Oh, for such a quick response on our part to the overt answers of God in our lives. To bow down, to rejoice, right there in the middle of the Lord's reply.

So often I don't even notice the answer, let alone remember to say a mere "Thank you." And rarely—OK, almost never—do I fall to my knees in thankful worship. God's response sneaks up on me, or I am charging full-throttle or have found something else to worry about (or pray about, on my better days). Or, perhaps, it seems a long, long time has elapsed before God can spare a response, and I've long given up on placing a check mark next to that item.

Maybe I've gone off on my own, using my internal GPS and mapping out my own path. You can't just stop moving, right, and sit around drumming your fingers on the arm of your easy chair, can you?

Besides, a relationship with God is so often private. Not everyone runs around sharing about God, about God's miraculous answers, about their trials and tribulations and all the ways they experience God's blessing. Not because their faith isn't real. But sometimes, there is no feel to faith. We have lived so long without a deep experience of God, without our hearts quickened by reading Scripture or praying or singing a hymn. We've waited for absolutely forever for answers. Sure, we plow ahead, we keep the faith, but we do so with our eyes on the road in front of us, the no-passing lines painted deep on our souls.

We don't really expect an answer, sometimes, after such a long wait, after so many nonanswers or outright "no, not now" or "no, not ever" responses.

I forget that all of those are actually answers: the wait, the no, the not now. They are also expressions of God's love for me, not God's lack of love. They represent God's favor or mercy . . . even God's blessing. Because blessing means God's provision for us in ways that fit us exactly: our personality, our circumstances. I'm beyond grateful that God knows more than I do, that God knows precisely what vital elements need to appear in my life, and when.

What if, as an experiment, we choose, today, to bow down and worship the Lord, maybe even get right down on our knees or throw ourselves prostrate on the floor? Even if we don't have an answer. Even if we don't see God's attentiveness and don't experience God's presence, we bend our knees and bend our hearts, offering a fumbling word of trust and worship.

We choose to worship God in the silence of God's not answering.

Isn't this the essence of faith?

TRAVELING MERCY

Dear one,
I may seem silent,
But I am actively
Listening
For your heart,
For your soul,
For your needs and wants.
And I have your best at heart.
Thank you for trusting me
Enough to worship me,
Even when you do not see
My hand.
I am here with you,
Loving you,
Even in the quiet.

NOTE TO SELF

Worship in spite of God's apparent silence.

THE LIST

Praise be to the LORD . . . who has not
abandoned his kindness and faithfulness.

—GENESIS 24:27

Have you made your list and placed it before God? A
clear, concise, "Here's how you can answer me" list that
leaves no doubt when it's answered. Maybe you have a long
list of unanswered pleas, urgent messages left in God's inbox
without response. Heartaches and heartbreaks that whisper or
even shout of abandonment by God, the God who is supposed
to have your best interests at heart.

But God doesn't always answer prayers as specifically as
in the case of Abraham's servant. We can't always check off
our prayer list items, drawing a line through all the requests
or adorning the list with exclamation points and stars and the
dates of fulfillment. How easy it would be to assume that God
has in fact abandoned us, or found someone with greater
needs than our own. True, others may have greater needs than
our own, that their hearts' desires might be weightier than our
own, as in life or death situations they may face. But other
people are not more important to God or higher in God's
esteem than we are.

In spite of every single evidence to the contrary—and there are many because we can't always see or hear God and can't always feel God nearby—God has not abandoned us. We may feel abandoned, but feelings are not our boss. We need to pay attention to that feeling of abandonment and then align it with what we know to be true about God.

God is faithful; we can take that faithfulness to the spiritual bank. Even when the entire world fails us, God is faithful (see Lam. 3:23).

God will not abandon us. "Never will I leave you, never will I forsake you" (Heb. 13:5). "Surely I am with you always, to the very end of the age" (Matt. 28:20).

Just because we feel abandoned or neglected or somewhere on the bottom of God's priority list, doesn't mean that's the truth. Rather than hold up our list of unanswered prayers as proof of God's abandonment, we could hold up Scripture as proof of God's faithfulness. And the more we examine our own lives, the more we notice God's presence, surprising us in unasked-for ways.

Maybe it's the phone call at the perfect time, or the birthday box from a friend that arrived six months late but at the exact moment you needed to feel loved. Maybe it's a word from someone who said, "God put you on my heart today," and today was the critical day for such affirmation.

Maybe we look and look and turn up blank—clueless detectives in sleuthing out God's presence. But that doesn't mean that abandonment is true.

The truth? Based on God's Word, whether or not someone shows up with a jug of water at the precise time we request it, we are not abandoned by God. God is faithful and will not abandon the work of his hands (see Ps. 138:8).

We can make our list. But we need to look not only for those things, but also for answers that may not be on that log. Answers that may be far better than anything we could have written on our tissue-paper lists. So we, too, can say with Abraham's servant, "Praise be to the Lord . . . who has not abandoned his kindness and faithfulness." Because that's the absolute truth.

TRAVELING MERCY
Dear one,
Abandonment
Is not in my vocabulary.
That's not what I do
With my children,
With you.
I will meet your needs.
I will provide what you need
To live,
Really live,
During this time.
And don't compare your list of answers
With someone else's list.
Watch for my kindness
And faithfulness.

NOTE TO SELF
I'll keep watch. God promised.

ABANDONMENT, IN OTHER WORDS

Praise be to the LORD, the God of my master Abraham,
who has not abandoned his kindness and faithfulness to my master.

—GENESIS 24:27

Abandonment is one of the most deadly feelings, having originated in Eden and leaves muddy footprints all over our souls and relationships ever since. Abandonment says that we are not loved, not tended to, not special, not cared for, and not on anyone's priority list. Abandonment whispers to us that we don't matter. That no one loves us, certainly not the most vital people in our lives.

Abandonment is one of the Evil One's greatest lies. Abandonment jerks us, away from community into isolation. That's the Enemy's turf, because isolation separates us from God and from people who could tell us the truth: that we are loved, that God formed us and called us from forever.

Abandoned also means "rejected, left destitute." How frequently is that our reaction and sensation—that we are destitute when we don't experience God's kindness and faithfulness in ways that register with our earthly senses?

Truly we are destitute without God, though all the voices in the world around us and even in our own heads insinuate or shout that we don't need God. That we can do this ourselves and can make a life on our own. That our stuff satisfies us, that we can find fulfillment in relationships, and that casual contacts and lots of technology connect and complete us.

But in the end, in our aloneness, we know the deeper truth: Without God, we are destitute. We have nothing and no one if we have not God. We have no hope, no certain future, no unending love. We may have food and shelter, but before long we recognize that without God, nothing matters and nothing makes sense. We're missing more than the biggest piece of the puzzle; we're missing the entire box with the full-color picture on the top.

Sometimes, in the depths of our despair, we desert God. God hasn't acted as we expected, hasn't answered like we thought, hasn't provided for us as we think we deserve. We've created God in our own image, and God hasn't cooperated.

Without God, our destitution leaves us feeling devastatingly alone. Without the light of God in our lives, we squat in the darkness of despair. And that feeling is true. Without God, we are destitute, alone, and despairing, though we stuff many fillers into the gaps.

But we cannot stop with that truth, because the truth is larger than this. Our feelings do not stop God's faithfulness.

Abraham's servant raised his arms in praise and threw himself to the ground in joy, in the freedom of abandon. "Praise be to the LORD . . . who has not abandoned his kindness and faithfulness," he shouted.

Whatever our dark, our sense of despair does not determine God's presence. God is the light that shines in the darkness, the One who overcomes the darkness with light. However deep the night, however many prayers on our list remain unanswered, we, too, shout the truth: Praise be to the Lord, who has not abandoned his kindness and faithfulness.

May God give us eyes to see in the dark.

TRAVELING MERCY
Dear one,
It's not always a walk in the park.
It's sometimes,
Or even often,
A walk in the dark,
But I will guide you.
You will see
I am the God who provides,
The God who sees
In the deep dark.

NOTE TO SELF
Night goggles, coming right up.

FOCUS

"Do not detain me."

—GENESIS 24:56

Rebekah's brother Laban and his household did all in their power to stop Abraham and Isaac's trusted servant from leaving. They wined and dined him, fed his camels and his traveling companions, and put them all up for the night. The hosts received, of course, all the gifts the servant brought, generous gifts from a foreign land. They logged in the gifts for Rebekah as well, finding no fault with any of it. In fact, the riches spread before them and all the jewelry bangling off Rebekah left them practically bug-eyed.

Still, they said, "Stay, oh, say, ten more days and let's see how all this goes."

The servant would have none of it. A man on a mission, he focused on his purpose for being there. "Do not detain me," he said, "now that the LORD has granted success" (Gen. 24:56). Of course the hospitality felt good for someone who'd traveled on camel for three hundred or more miles. What relief, to put up his feet, relish hot food, and relax in Bethuel and Milkah's home.

But he refused to be detoured from his purpose. He came for a bride for his master's son, Isaac, and now that he'd found her, it was time to return home. He did not care about their opinions of him or his timetable. He focused on his journey's fulfillment.

The trusted family servant brought God into the discussion. Because his master's faith had become his own throughout the years, he knew without doubt that God had directed his very steps, right down to where he stood at the spring and the appropriate time of day to meet the right person.

It's easy to get sidetracked with the trappings—there's a good reason for that word—of success. But the servant stayed focused on his purpose, which didn't include an extended stay in the guest suites, being delayed (and played) by the bride's family. Besides, his job wasn't finished. He had many miles to travel with precious cargo—the bride, her maid, and all their belongings. His responsibility was great, and finding her was just the beginning. His masters were likely posted on the highest hill watching for their caravan's return. He couldn't afford to dally. People he loved and served waited for him.

Nor can we afford to get sidetracked from our course by the appearance or reality of success in an endeavor. Success is temporary this side of heaven: We follow the course until we achieve the next milestone, and then we saddle the camels and start the next leg of our journey. The resting place remains simply that: a temporary stop to recuperate with food and water, and a warm bath and bed. But ASAP, we get up and load up and head out. Refreshed, rested, and ready for the next milestone.

Perhaps we are loathe to acknowledge milestones for fear that we appear aggressive or proud. Yet they provide landmarks, goals, and opportunities to praise God. Just don't linger there, hindered by the world's temporary comfort. People who achieve great things for God do so because they keep their faces pointed toward heaven. That's when they achieve true success after all: when God calls them home.

Celebrate the success, by all means. Stop and give God glory and praise! And then get back on the camel. People are waiting for the good news.

TRAVELING MERCY

Dear one,
So glad you've noticed.
So happy you're pleased.
And I'm so happy to please you.
Put your feet up and rest a bit.
But know when to stay
And when to go.
Don't be swayed by luxury
Or even by simple hospitality.
Saddle up.
It's about time
To ride.

NOTE TO SELF

Rest up and then ride on.

THE INTERMEDIARY

"The LORD has granted success to my journey."

—GENESIS 24:56

"The Lord has granted success," the servant said, as he recapped the journey's outcome to Rebekah's family. He took no credit for his own skills of bride selection or diplomacy. He could have felt a puff of pride: he was, after all, Abraham's most trusted servant. And, considering how the mission played out, he could have thought: "Look at how wisely and brilliantly I prayed, look at the perfect timing of my arrival, look at how wonderfully the bride's family received the gifts . . . look, look, look at how well this has gone on my account. I must be special because God answers my prayers."

But the servant didn't. His servanthood was far more than a mere job, a clocking in and clocking out of Abraham's household. Rather, day after day of faithfulness to Abraham and his needs instilled in this man the nature of a servant. Serving became his trademark. It was his character, and he recognized his role: a go-between. Between God and Isaac, between Abraham and the fulfilling of God's promise to him, between Isaac and his future, and between Rebekah and her family, the almost in-laws.

His attitude was so . . . well, Christlike. Christ, who assumed the form of a servant. Christ, the go-between for us—between us and God, us and salvation, us and heaven. He still is, constantly interceding for us with God for the best in our lives and the rest of our lives.

An intermediary. What if we would see ourselves forever as intermediaries between others and God, others and salvation, others and heaven? Between others and their futures? With this viewpoint, any success traveling our way simply forwards God's goals in others' lives, as well as in our own. With this outlook, we recognize every interaction as an opportunity for us to convey God's love and kindness to others.

If interactions are opportunities to convey love, we see any interruption as an intersection, a place of meeting and potential mediation. Any unexpected encounter, any unexpected (or hoped for) success becomes an interception: God intercepting others' lives with the opportunity for us to be a go-between.

Then, no matter what errands send us out, we can always pray as the servant prayed, "Lord, God . . . if you will, please grant success to the journey on which I have come." We faithfully log our miles and follow God's lead and directions. And as long as we keep our focus on the point of our journey—that we are God's intermediaries and that we help bridge the gap between heaven and earth, between today and tomorrow for everyone we meet—then we can conclude with the servant's prayer, as well: "The Lord has granted success to my journey."

TRAVELING MERCY
Dear one,
I'm delighted
At your servant heart
And grateful
That you recognize yourself
As a go-between.
You represent me
Everywhere you go,
And people make decisions about faith,
And about me,
When they meet you.
So love well
And pay close attention
To every seeming interruption.
I love a successful ending.

NOTE TO SELF
Interruptions are actually interceptions.

A RESOUNDING YES

"I will go."
—Genesis 24:58

The blessing rang in her ears, and currents of anticipation and fear pricked her heart. As her family waved her off, Rebekah mounted her camel. She plodded through the wilderness, knowing full well that she might never see her parents again and might never again experience her brother's protection over her. She might never trek the familiar trail to the river for water in the evening. She might never return with her children to show them her childhood home and let them meet their grandparents and uncle. She might never get to say, "And here is where my life changed. Here is where I began a journey with the one true God. Here is where I said yes to an adventure that changed my entire life."

What if she'd said, "No, thanks. Intriguing, of course, but I like my watering routine day and night, trekking to the river with my heavy jug, filling it, hefting it overhead, and returning home. I like my life the way it is. I'm comfortable here, if a little bored, but no, seriously, really, no thanks"? What if she'd shut the door on the possibility that God beckoned?

God can always find someone else to answer the door. In fact, God constantly knocks on doors, rings doorbells, and climbs in through windows to invite people into life. But when God knocks on *my* life, I want to say yes. Yes! A resounding yes.

This doesn't have to be impetuous. Rebekah weighed all the evidence. She heard the servant's story, his prayers, and the background of his master. No doubt she liked the jewelry, but there could be no coincidence given the facts: He'd asked God for the right woman to first give him water and then to water all the camels. She couldn't get over it: His master was her great uncle, the man Abraham, who'd left a million years before she was born to follow his God to who knows where.

Imagine that! What are the chances that she'd be the first one to show up that night at the spring, the first one the servant spoke to?

In spite of overwhelming evidence, she still sought counsel, a wise choice for any of us, but essential in her culture. She sought the counsel of those who knew her, knew how she approached life, how she handled responsibility. Knew her character. They agreed to the adventure, provided that she felt secure in saying yes.

And we can do the same. Review the evidence. Consult key people who know us and love us and want the best for us. And then, we join the resounding chorus of people through the centuries who have raised their hands and shouted, "I will go!"

TRAVELING MERCY
Dear one,
Knock knock.
Who's there, you ask?
It is I Aм.
And I'm here to ask you
For a date—
For an adventure of a lifetime.
Will you say yes?
We are perfect
For each other.

NOTE TO SELF
Today, can I say, "I will go"?

THE YES THAT CHANGES THE WORLD

"I'm ready to go."

—GENESIS 24:58 MSG

Rebekah's yes in response to her brother, her parents, and the servant didn't just change her life. Her yes changed the lives of her maids, parents, and brother. It changed the servant's life. (He might have been next in line for the inheritance had Isaac been without a bride.)

In fact, to be bold about it all: Rebekah's yes changed the world. Her simple statement, "I will go," continued the momentum of God's promise to a longing world: "I will bless you and make you a blessing" (see Gen. 12:1–4).

And isn't every single day a day that might change our entire lives? A day that might, in a miraculous heavenly reality, change the world? Maybe we don't settle onto a saddle on a camel's back, but every day that we awaken from sleep, we can say yes to adventure, yes to God, and yes to all the surprises coming our way that day. Rebekah could have said a flat no to change, and so can we. But why say no?

Fear of the unknown, perhaps? Rebekah might have stayed put with her ultimately scheming brother and remained under his thumb. She could have said yes to sameness, because the known sometimes, or often, feels safer than the vast horizons of the unknown. Launching off on a long bumpy trip with an unknown servant and a herd of camels could have been threatening to a girl back then—or now, for that matter.

Fear makes too many decisions for us. Rebekah refused to let fear cast the deciding vote in her life's journey—and in the journey of a lifetime. She couldn't overlook the infusion of hope that interrupted the sameness of her days and nights. She couldn't allow the fear to win.

If fear decides, regret inevitably trails behind with its mammoth stomping feet.

The next time adventure rides up into the middle of your daily drag, whether via a camel or phone call or e-mail or knock at the front door or the door of your heart, don't send fear to answer for you. Consider the indicators God sends. Invite clarity and wisdom. By all means decide soundly.

Besides, we might not even have to leave home. Because every single day we say yes to God, we say yes to adventure. Rather than suffer a lifetime of fear mingled with the bitterness of regret, live and leave a legacy of adventure.

That's some serious inheritance. The yes that changes the world.

TRAVELING MERCY
Dear one,
Fear makes for
Bad decisions.
So wait to say yes,
But don't wait too long.
Time's a wastin'
And we have miles to travel
Together,
You and I.
Sights to see.
Adventures to live.
Say yes?

NOTE TO SELF

Don't let fear answer the door.

THE LINE OF BLESSING

And they blessed Rebekah.

—GENESIS 24:60

As Rebekah prepared to leave, Laban and her mother gathered about Rebekah, willing at last to send her away to Uncle Abraham's only son. That sending off can be a visceral pain.

Last week, I told my parents good-bye. Outside, a For Sale sign protruded from their yard. Their walkers and canes rested near the dining room table like loyal companions as I bent to kiss my dad. He rose, always a gentleman, for a real and proper hug. He is much shorter now than in his younger years, life taking its toll on his back, but his embrace is still so comforting.

I turned toward my mother and leaned down for a hug. She said to my father, "Honey, say a prayer over Jane."

My dad moved to my side and reached for my hand. His hands, once so clever with a pen and so strong and big and vital from hefting oil drums, hauling, and working physically hard. Now, his fingers were bent and nobbled as they gripped my own.

And my mother's hands, so capable and strong, sewing and embroidering, cooking, gardening, lithe with accounting and numbers, nimble with words, and now with swollen knuckles and thin skin. She grasped my right hand, and we bowed our heads.

Many miles after backing down my parents' driveway and away from my childhood home, the simple and surprising holiness of our tiny circle at the dining room table surrounds me. This rare gift of blessing allowed me to leave with both tears and peace, re-centering my hopes on the God who provides and who protects me and my parents.

Leaving. Life is full of leavings. Parting from friends, family, traditions, the comfort of routine, and even the discomfort of all those relationships. To leave cleanly, to leave with hope, we could pray a blessing and covering over both the ones who leave and the ones who stay behind.

Whether we are the ones left or the ones who leave, we can offer a blessing. Whether we were raised with a family blessing or raised outside of any sense of blessing whatsoever, now is a perfect time to begin a new tradition. Whether people expect a blessing or have never experienced the surprise of a prayer prayed over them in benediction, it's never too late. We enter into an ancient practice when we step into the midst of an invocation and invite God's covering and presence over people we love.

Last week, I left my parents. This week, from the other side of the country, I left my daughter, her husband, and their baby daughter and boarded a flight home. Next week, I will leave a son in another state and the following week, a son in yet a third state. All far away geographically yet connected by the fine, common filament of blessing, some spoken, some unspoken, all heart-felt.

The leavings will continue for the rest of our lives, people leaving us, us leaving others. Until the last trumpet sounds, we will be people who come and go, always seeking the next destination. May we lift our hearts toward heaven, pull heaven toward earth, and bless and bless and bless.

Whether we part in sorrow or joy, we part in peace and hope, carrying the blessing forward into the world.

"And they blessed Rebekah." May it be so with us.

TRAVELING MERCY

Dear one,
One person
Plus me
Creates a circle of blessing.
So if no one else joins you,
I am there blessing
Those you bless.
Leave well.
Leave with peace.
Leave blessing.
And leave the ones you love
To me and my love.
Don't be afraid
To pray a blessing.
People are dying
For that kind of love,
That circle of hope.

NOTE TO SELF

I can start a habit of blessing others aloud!

JULY DEVOTIONS

WATERING HOLE

Now Isaac had come from Beer Lahai Roi.

—GENESIS 24:62

While the servant caravans toward home with Rebekah, Isaac enters the scene stage left, from the vicinity of a well, "From *Beer Lahai Roi*," which means, "well of the living one who sees me."

Isaac, for reasons known only to him, decided to live in the Negev, a relatively undesirable section of the Promised Land. The word *Negev* comes from a Hebrew word meaning "south," and this desert region in the southern section covers more than 55 percent of the land of Israel.[1] That's a lot of desert. And a lot of desert means barrenness and a lack of obvious water sources.

Flora and fauna figure out how to live in the desert. Some of the roots of desert plants grow twenty feet deep so they can access any possible underground water. Other desert plants have broad roots that spread out along the surface of the soil for maximum exposure and intake of any moisture, whether dew, humidity, or actual rainfall. In the Negev, situated due east of the Sahara, rainfall averages between four and twelve inches per year.

For human beings, survival in the wilderness requires deliberate effort and desert wisdom. Water obviously is the life-or-death element physically. If you're going to live in the desert, you need to find a well, like Isaac did, the "well of the living one who sees me."

And spiritually, too, we need to find a well. Figuring out where to plant ourselves is critical for lasting, let alone blooming, in desert places. And who of us hasn't been in the desert, hasn't felt like the Sahara lives right next door? Maybe you've been in the wilderness more than 55 percent of the time, for years that seem to dwarf the size of the Negev.

Where is your well? Where do you find rest for your soul? Where is your oasis?

A well in the desert, a well specific to your love-language, your places of greatest receptivity to God's presence. Where do you experience God's presence? Find yourself a well. And drink deeply. You'll be glad you did. And so will your people.

TRAVELING MERCY
Dear one,
You wouldn't hike in the desert
Without water,
So don't hike in the wilderness of life
Without knowing where you'll find
Wells.
Notice your thirst
And how to slake your parched life.
I can lead you to water,
But you have to choose to drink.

NOTE TO SELF

What well will I visit this day?

NOTE

1. Wikipedia, "Negev," last updated August 26, 2014, http://en.wiki
pedia.org/wiki/Negev.

JULY 2

REAL LIFE

[Isaac] was living in the Negev.

—Genesis 24:62

Because of his locale, Isaac knew that, only after too-close encounters, do you recognize the enemy's many faces. Whether a mountain lion, skin-melting heat, or ferocious wind, the enemy reveals its dangerous presence. But sometimes, the enemy is invisible, because the enemy is you.

In the movie *The Edge*, Anthony Hopkins's character says that most people lost in the wilderness die of shame.[1] Shame, because we pound ourselves with questions like, how could I have let this happen? How did I lose my way? Lose control? Lose sight . . . lose my map . . . lose? And before long, we are so focused on ourselves that we stop thinking clearly.

How we came to be in the wilderness is important. It might help us retrace our steps so we can get out. But self-flagellation rarely aids navigation in the barrens. It's a poor compass, though it's admittedly one of my personal favorite tools of ineffective guidance.

If it's not shame, then blame can take us down. It's worse than a rattlesnake for immobilization, poisoning our souls and our survival chances. Blaming others for where we are, where we aren't, how we are, how we aren't. How they are, or aren't, or were, or weren't.

Both shame and blame divert our attention and focus away from the challenge of survival. It's good to know why we're in the hardscrabble space—perhaps knowing it will prevent us from a repeat dilemma. But the wilderness requires action rather than reaction. Thoughtfulness, not impulse.

From what we can see of Isaac's life, and of Ishmael's life for that matter, blame and shame weren't part of the game plan. Isaac moved into adulthood with responsibilities intact, and even when he moved to the Negev, he navigated those lands well. He married Rebekah, the woman God found for him, and raised two lively and bright sons. He continued to believe in and build into the promise that God made to his father, and then to him and to his boys after him.

Ultimately, the Scriptures tell us, Isaac knew the wilderness wasn't his inheritance, nor the tents he lived in, nor all that he received from his parents, both good and bad. Rather, he found his inheritance in the faithfulness of God, who saved him and led him into a spacious place. His inheritance would be found, not in a city of brick and mortar, of stone foundations, but rather in a city invisible to the earthly eye (see Heb. 11:9).

How tempting to keep count by looking at our past or to fixate on the altar moments when we felt at another's mercy, like Isaac. Or to tally our grievances and slights. Had Isaac lived like that, perhaps he never would have married, never would have carried on the promise made to his father. Instead, he focused on passing along the blessing, on sealing the next generation for the life God had in store for them.

Keeping focus in the wilderness does more than save our lives. It prepares us, and helps us prepare others, for real life, abundant life. Forever life. We have to keep the blessing moving forward.

TRAVELING MERCY
Dear one,
Shame, blame, and
More of the same.
Stop that game and start,
Instead,
To think smart
So you can move forward
With your life
And helps others move
Along with theirs.
Your altars are real and difficult,
But begin to heal
So you can keep that life
Rolling on and out.

NOTE TO SELF
Today I will own my responsibility for my life.

NOTE
1. *The Edge*, directed by Lee Tamahori (Venice, CA: Art Linson Productions, 1997), DVD.

PERSPECTIVE

He went out to the field one evening to meditate.

—Genesis 24:63

Isaac hoped that very soon his father's trusted servant would return, knowing that his life might change in dramatic ways and his responsibility expand greatly. He knew that the expectations upon him would likely increase monumentally, and soon. But in spite of all that coming pressure, or perhaps because of it, he walked out into the field one fine evening to meditate.

To meditate in the evening. We could call this verse, "How to end the day well." Except the Hebrew people start the day with sundown, so perhaps it's, "How to begin the day well." How to shed the stress of the day and invite the gift of respite to begin its healing.

The three patriarchs in Jewish history are noted for different attributes. Abraham is renowned for hospitality. For Jacob, it's balance, the ability to bridge the divide. Some historians attribute to Isaac the gift of spirituality and the origin of evening prayer. He is the contemplative one, based on a fairly quiet life and this note in Genesis 24:63.

But this isn't just Old Testament stuff, something to admire from a long-ago era. The implications are significant for our physical and mental, as well as our spiritual, health. Scanning the vast horizons, the open land, the crops; listening to the wind, to the silence behind the wind, to the wordlessness of our own heart. Wide-open spaces whisper or shout possibility and hope. The vastness reminds us of our smallness, and either leads us to hopelessness, or to the hope that God is behind the largeness of creation.

Morning, evening, middle of the day — anytime is a good time to consider. To meditate. To take stock of yourself, your day, your place in the time-space continuum, and your God. It's a means of re-centering, or coming back to the core of yourself. To ask: Where am I, in terms of faith? Where am I, in terms of living today in God's presence? Where have I sensed God's presence? Where have I bypassed God's presence and ruptured relationships?

This assessment tool helps us step outside of our own craziness, outside of our toxic schedules and stress. It helps us step outside of our limited and self-focused lives, to see the bigger picture of the big world around us, and the One who holds the whole world — including us — in very capable and compassionate hands.

Perhaps this is why the psalmist says, "I lift up my eyes to the mountains — where does my help come from?" (Ps. 121:1). Away from our days, away from our mistakes and disappointments, and toward God. Whether traipsing out to the field in the evening, shoving away from our desk at lunch, or turning our hearts toward God from the rumpled beds of our life, we look toward heaven. We gaze at the wide-open grace of this God who loves us, who called us out of obscurity, who singled us out for a relationship made in eternity past.

And there, in that space, we are safe. We are loved. We can rest. Tomorrow, after all, is another day. And meanwhile, God is still God.

TRAVELING MERCY

Dear one,
Take a deep breath,
Lift up your eyes,
Smell the cut grass,
Watch the twinkling star-life
In the night sky,
Breathe into the darkness
And hear my word for you.
Your days are crowded
With fear and insufficiency
And your nights
With more anxiety.
You will never finish your work,
But you can start or finish the day strong
By turning toward me,
Trusting me,
For I am the God who
Formed you.
I am the God who loves you.
Come to me.

NOTE TO SELF

Stepping out in the evening to meditate.
I will try this, and live.

IMPOSSIBLE INHERITANCE

He went out to the field one evening to meditate.

—Genesis 24:63

Isaac, the middleman in the new clan of Abraham. He would forward the family line and propel it into a great nation, a blessed people whose primary purpose was to bless others. That's a lot to saddle a kid with. He'd inherited more than his father's business acumen or his mother's fine looks; more than the material goods Abraham accumulated during his long and prosperous 175-year lifetime.

Many only children report that the expectations on them as their parents' sole legacy and heir weighed—still weighs— heavily on them. Parents naturally invest hopes and dreams as well as material goods and time into their children, and all that heaped onto one child can be an amazing gift. It can lead to rare and precious privileges, education, and opportunities. And we all need to be the center of attention at times, to know that we exist on our own merit as individuals.

Such attention can also be overwhelming. We all know parents who try to live vicariously through their offsprings' achievements—parents who push their child to excel at dreams belonging more to parent than to child. Whether sports or hobbies or academic courses, when parents force special interests on their children it can lead to despair for the kids.

What of Isaac's interior life? Everything depended on him, it would seem. And what sorts of mental gyrations and gymnastics had he developed to process his relationship with his own parents? But it's part of the work of growing up, of growing into our inheritance in constructive ways, so that rather than beat up on our parents, we do our own work. Sorting out who we are, in light of the parenting we received, and choosing how to live into that inheritance well, becomes a major work of adulthood. The people who sign up for that course choose a messy but ultimately fruitful route.

Perhaps that's why, at this encounter, we find Isaac in the field in the evening. Meditating.

Without that space, some place of endless sky and immensity, we lose perspective. From his grounded spot on the earth he tended, as he gazed up into the open vista, Isaac could re-center. The God who called his father from obscurity into a blessing, called Isaac as well. Here, he could remember that calling. Here, he could embrace the marvelous impossibilities because the creation of the God of the impossible surrounded him.

Here, with the sun setting and a mist rising from the ground; here, with the stars peeping from their hiding spots like tiny torches as the daylight faded, Isaac could remember: His inheritance depended not on the fallibility or inscrutable ways of his parents, not on his own degree of woundedness or giftedness—and perhaps wounds and gifts are proportionate—but rather, on his God.

May it be so for us, as well: children of the inheritance, the unlikely heirs of earth (and all the complications of humanity) and the delightfully impossible heirs of the God of the impossible.

TRAVELING MERCY
Dear one,
Evening or morning
Come to me.
You will see a world
Far bigger than your life can hold.
But know that I can hold your life
Just fine,
And I long to give you more and more
Of my own.
So find a field,
Any field,
And open yourself
To heaven.
You will live longer,
But more importantly you will live
With me
Well.

NOTE TO SELF
I am the heir of the God of the impossible.
That should do it for today.

DWELLING

He went out . . . to meditate.

—Genesis 24:63

However Isaac filled his days as a man of wealth in the era of 1800 BC, in the evening, he called a ceasefire and went to the field to meditate.

Somewhere in our lives there must be places of quiet, where our overbearing brain doesn't outshout our soul. Places to set aside time on a regular basis to listen and to be still. *Meditate* can mean to "dwell upon" something, and in our treadmill-paced lives, we dwell seldom. In fact, in some areas of the United States we dwell in one place for less than two years before moving on to another dwelling.

Without dwelling places, we live without roots. And Isaac, who lived in the desert area of Negev, needed roots. Deep roots, to tap into the nourishment available to him. He needed depth, not shallow and dry surface sustenance.

Our society expects us to live on the half-inch of topsoil of the world: the eye candy, the tech thrills. Just ask around: Someone will have a new product guaranteed to help you feel better, at least in the moment of consumption. But a steady diet of any of these fillers renders us weak and shaking, like we've just ridden three days in a car and swallowed gallons of coffee and repeated shots of straight caffeine from the gas stations along the way but ate no real food.

But to dwell, to meditate, to stay in one place and consider? How do we dwell when our entire life is like the Los Angeles rush hour? When our brain is a five-point intersection with no traffic lights and strings of thoughts all lined up waiting for passage?

Dwelling requires slowing down. Dwelling needs time. Dwelling takes practice.

When my children were young, they occasionally needed a time-out in order to slow down, process their emotions, or distance themselves from a heated sibling exchange. Time to think without distraction about their part in the fight. As they grew older, we initiated a 30-30-30 time for each summer day. Not as punishment, though they never believed that at the time. Thirty minutes each of reading, journaling, and music or art. Then they were free to run, play, and build. They universally loathed these minutes set aside for their own slow, their own dwelling.

Today, however, they tell us it was a good practice, this self-feeding of the mind and heart and soul. Deliberate self-care is not automatic for most of us. It's an acquired taste. Once we begin to experience the benefits of dwelling, the gift of standing in the field at the end, or beginning, of a long day, we recognize that truly "the earth is the Lord's and the fullness thereof." To stand in the field, like Isaac, meditating. Dwelling space.

TRAVELING MERCY
Dear one,
Dwell deep
And you will dwell well.
Love,
God.

NOTE TO SELF

What would 30-30-30 look like in my life?

A DEEP BREATH

Trust in the LORD, and do good.
Dwell in the land and enjoy safe pasture.

—PSALM 37:3

Isaac's challenge, Esau and Jacob's after him, and ours as well, is to live here, where we are, right now. To pay attention to the present moment, fully aware of ourselves, our surroundings, and our God. It's no small feat, but paying attention is the only way to stay alive in our ceaselessly moving world.

Right *now* is where we meet God. In this minute of our day. Here's one way to dwell in the moment: Like Isaac, breathe in the evening air—or the moist morning fog, or the breeze that rustles past the lilies or blooming hostas. Fill your lungs with more than the exhaust fumes of your life and your neighbor's hot rod.

I run through much of my day not smelling anything, not because I can't, but because I grew up in a smoke-filled, cigarette-burning America where smoke constantly wafted. I trained myself to breathe through my mouth so I didn't sneeze. Not smelling aromas works well for unpleasant smells, and sometimes even stops the gag reflex for extremely sensitive smellers. Still, in general, it's not a good practice.

Smelling is a rich and vital sense, adding another dimension to our lives, but also to our souls. I need to unlearn this mouth-breathing technique, because it has outlived its usefulness for 90 percent of my waking life.

Dinnertime was a sacred time in our home as my husband and I raised our children, and I fought against deadlines and the brood's competing commitments in order to have a savory meal ready to carry to the table when our family at last gathered from their long days. My heart always leaped when a child burst through the door and slid to a hockey-stop halt, shouting, "Something smells soooo good."

Basil and sage plants grow in my garden, along with far too many tomato plants. I love to jiggle the leaves and then breathe in, slowly. The fresh herbs and the tangy scent of the tomato vines smell like hope to me, and life.

Try this. Breathe through your nose, so you can smell. What do you smell? Like a chef tasting a mystery dish, try to identify the ingredients in the aromas filling you. In that moment of appreciation of aroma, we are truly alive. Awareness of the world around us helps us dwell, and when we dwell, we can move in praise into God's presence.

Go ahead. Take a deep breath of the world around you.

Now, shift your breathing focus. One of the names for the Holy Spirit in the original language is Breath. Fill your lungs with a deep draught of the Holy Spirit. Seriously, stop what you're doing and deliberately breathe deeply. Do this again, consciously inviting the Holy Spirit to breathe God's breath in you, expanding throughout your system, the oxygen of God's power coursing through your bloodstream.

   Suddenly, we are Isaac, filling our lungs with the rich layered scents of creation, participating in our inheritance, as children born anew into the family of God. It's called living. It's called dwelling.

TRAVELING MERCY
Dear one,
Smell the world around you.
Some lovely aromas,
And some not,
But breathe anyway.
You will stay alive.
And let me breathe my breath
Into you,
Just like creation's
Dawn.
Inhale until you are full
And then hold.
Exhale.
Repeat.

NOTE TO SELF
Deep breath. Smell the world around you.

BACKWARD TO THE PROMISE, FORWARD TO THE BLESSING

In the evening . . . while meditating . . .
—Genesis 24:63 msg

News of a move landed like the morning paper, smack in the middle of major deadlines and personal headlines. "I don't have time to worry about moving now. Next week," I thought. Next week I could worry? I laughed to even think about scheduling my worries for a more convenient timeframe.

Rounding the bend of heavy commitments, I collapsed on the sofa early Sunday morning, Bible, journal, and lectionary all in my lap. As the sun rose, I gulped in the glory and the open time like a train passenger suddenly freed from the steam engine's choking smoke. But then, just as I caught my breath, a train wreck of postponed worries piled up on me: Where would we live? Six weeks to physically pack our home, two offices, and an attic filled with family history? How do we keep up with our ministry commitments *and* pack *and* find a new place to live *and* still have time to sleep?

And then, I repeated to myself, "Where will we go?" Scratch off "sleep." No time for that or we'd be homeless.

Turning to the lectionary, the first reading listed Genesis 12:1–4. "No, no, no. I know that one. I am not reading that. I'm through with Abraham. I need Isaac, Rebekah, and the twins now." But there it sat, the first passage in the four daily readings waiting for me. With a sigh, I flipped to that page, which is conveniently falling apart at the binding in my Bible.

I've memorized this passage, mulled over it, and written about it. Maybe like Isaac, who heard it day after day from his father Abraham, from birth onward. "This is what God told me, son, all those years ago, and this is what I've been handing down to you now all these years."

But never had I known the passage given the current parameters of my life: moving to a location undisclosed in a time too short to manage. And crowding onto that were regrets of the past years, too much hard work and under-fun, the toll on our family. The regrets battered at the door like masked thieves.

Beneath my protest about rereading a passage I already knew, about needing something new to run on, it occurred to me that surely Isaac, in all his uncertainties, kept returning to the promise God made to his father and to him. Surely reviewing God's promises in the past is critical to our momentum forward.

So I read the designated and familiar verses again. Out loud, which changes everything about my receptivity. "Leave," God said. "Your home, your people, your family's household." *Leave.* I swallowed. Yes, that was the word we'd heard this week. Tears choked my throat as I tried to squeeze the Scripture past. Leave, and then, "Go."

Go. In the Hebrew, *lekh lekha*, meaning, "to break, part ways with." To break with our history, our past, all the memories good and bad. To leave and go.

But then the words that fluttered with hope like party confetti in the midst of all the breaking and parting of ways: "To the land I will show you." Not "I might show you," but "I will show you." God said *will*, not *might*. I hold tightly to that, even as we explore options and create timelines and buy packing tape and collect boxes like the stars of a hoarders show. "To the land I will show you."

Even that isn't the end of the command: so that God can bless us and we can be a blessing. What more could I ask? Isn't that the whole point of our existence? God gave us life in order to bless us—showing incredible, undeserved love to us—so that we can bless others.

I open my hands in a receiving gesture. Bring it on, Lord. I'll pack while you figure out where we're going. Just let us be a blessing, wherever we land.

Sometimes we have to meditate on what we already know, so we can move forward armed for what we do not yet see.

TRAVELING MERCY

Dear one,
The promise to Abraham,
To Isaac,
To Jacob,
Holds for you,
Because you are part of my family now.
So leave and go,
And remember what I said;
"To the land I will show you."
Whether a literal new place to land
Or a new thought or relationship,
I will show you,
Because I always keep my word.

NOTE TO SELF

Be free to go along into the new.

A TASTE OF PERSONALITY

Esau said to Jacob, "Quick, let me have some
of that red stew! I'm famished!"

—GENESIS 25:30

Isaac lifted his gaze from the fields and saw the caravan approaching. His heart leaped. The servant had returned, and—wait—who was the woman with the veil over her face?

He ran to meet his new bride, and, like many, they began their marriage with great hope. His relationship with Rebekah comforted him, and he began to heal from so many losses. Life had proven costly thus far, but now, surely, the two of them together would raise a gaggle of children and carry on the sacred covenant that God gave to Abraham. But then, almost twenty years into marriage, Rebekah still was not pregnant. Isaac took to his knees, took to the fields, and took his prayers to the God of his father. He begged God to open his wife's womb.

Rebekah at last conceived, but the pregnancy involved a civil war in her womb. In misery, she asked God, "Why is this happening to me?" (see Gen. 25:19–26).

God said, "Two nations are in your womb, and two peoples from within you will be separated; one people will be stronger than the other, and the older will serve the younger."

Twins! The part about serving, Rebekah didn't yet understand. But she would play a starring role in the prophecy's fulfillment.

At the children's births, their names, as usual, described the surrounding circumstances. The firstborn made his grand entrance, entirely red, his whole body like a hairy coat. But before Esau cleared the birth canal, his younger brother grabbed onto Esau's heel en route to freedom. Enter child number two, Jacob, "he grasps the heel," a Hebrew idiom for "he who deceives."

The children grew, as did their tastes. Esau loved hunting, "a man of the open country." Jacob contented himself around the tents.[1] Isaac loved hunting wild game, and Esau became his favorite son. Rebekah loved Jacob.

And so their family doubled in size. The tumbling boys grew to manhood, and their personalities grew, becoming legendary in Scripture. Esau hunted, Jacob cooked, and Rebekah stirred the pot.

One day, Esau tore into the tents, famished after a long day of hunting. At the scent of Jacob's stew, Esau exclaimed, "I'm dying! Feed me!" (see Gen. 25:27–34).

Hunger demands our attention, and that fateful day, Esau succumbed to hunger and handed over any common sense. He would replay this day in his mind for many years.

Jacob, of course, long knew that his birth order meant a disadvantage. The firstborn received a huge perk with the birthright. A double inheritance for the privilege and responsibility of caring for the family and their needs, including his mother, should she outlive Isaac, and any other relatives in need of care.

Recognizing an opportunity, Jacob cooked up a deal that any Wall Street wizard would envy: a bowl of stew for the birthright. Esau's appetite ruled him thoroughly; he didn't even question the wisdom of the trade. Talk about appetites! Jacob's hunger for authority and power, and Esau's hunger for food and immediate satisfaction.

We are no different. Our appetite consistently begs us for appeasement: settle down those growling pains, all that internal rumbling, with position or possessions or people. Maybe we, too, are both Jacob and Esau, a civil war within us, constantly asking for meaning and satiation.

Esau's capitulation hints at the makings of depravity. A man ruled by his cravings rather than his responsibility as firstborn son. The birthright, according to Jewish tradition, also included spiritual leadership. Remember Abraham in intimate conversations with the Lord and the impact of his spirituality on his servant, who prayed and praised God? And Isaac, meditating in a field at the end of a long day?

One more reason to pay attention, to dwell deeply. Perhaps then we at least have a chance at recognizing our true hunger when it appears.

TRAVELING MERCY
Dear one,
Hunger will always fight
For your heart,
So aim your heart
Toward me,
And we will work together
To sort out your hungers.
Remember that without exception
Your deepest hunger
Is for unending,
Unfailing,
Love.

NOTE TO SELF

Notice hunger and point it to God.

NOTE

1. It's possible that the tents referred to are shepherds' tents, moveable camps set up while a flock grazed in that location. Jacob, as chef, would have authority over any food given away there, even to his own brother. It is also possible that if Esau was the hunter, then Jacob was the shepherd, which would account for his expertise with sheep later.

HUNGER THE HUNTER

"Look, I am about to die. . . . What good is the birthright to me?"
—GENESIS 25:32

Jacob, the quiet twin, stayed close to the tents. He proved to be quite a chef, stirring up a mean batch of stew and baking bread that drew people in from the fields, salivating. One day, the aroma of rich food wafted across the land to Esau, who became, instantly, ravenously hungry. And dramatic.

He hurtled into the compound, certain the doorknob of death's door turned for him. "Quick," he ordered his brother. "I'm famished. Serve me some of that soup!"

Ingenious Jacob recognized his opportunity and struck fast. "Absolutely. A trade. First you give me your birthright. Then you get your bowl of stew."

"I'm going to die here and now. I'm starving to death. I swear it. You can have my birthright. It's no good to me if I'm dead." And Esau, starving Esau, forked over his birthright for a spoonful of soup.

Hunger addles our brain, literally, according to research. Our blood sugar drops, and we do crazy things in our irrational state, like argue, fight, and commit crimes. But hunger also renders us delirious with ridiculous drama. Esau wasn't dying. He was hungry.

In our hunger, we strike bargains with people who might use our weakness against us. Esau, strong, hunter Esau, man of the bow and arrow, who did more than bring home the proverbial bacon—he shot and killed it, then hauled the animal back to the tents. He was strong of body but weak, perhaps, of resolve. Jacob, in a friendly world, complemented his brother's shortcomings. In their world of sibling rivalry, Jacob took advantage of his brother's weakness.

Good leaders do not allow their hunger to own them, to drive them to negative consequences. Good leaders see hunger as a gift, an edge, a tool that sharpens and directs their focus and skills. They capitalize on their hunger rather than allow it to control them. The inability to control hunger—whether lust for power or people or possessions—has led to the downfall of many visionaries and leaders, both in the world and in Christian circles. Esau, ruled by his hunger, forfeited his role in the family and in the future.

No one wants to be physically hungry, especially if that hunger cannot be easily or quickly satisfied before becoming painful. In our culture today, healthy hunger masquerades as necessity demanding immediate fulfillment. Like Esau, we want our stew and we want it today. Like Eve, who looked at the fruit and saw that it was pleasing to the eye and profitable to make her knowledgeable, we look, we want, we seize. Whatever dulls the pain, delays the inevitable, or distracts us, we consume.

Esau, the strong hunter, capitulated to his hunger and lost his birthright. He gave up his tomorrow for his today. It's the shortest of short-term plans, with an outcome so easily preventable. We can *tsk-tsk* poor Esau and shake our heads in our superiority. But we have done the same: We opt for entertainment rather than depth in a relationship, or gossip away to a friend because it's easier than dealing with the situation firsthand. We, too, have paid dearly to have our needs, both tangible and intangible, satisfied. The cost? A chunk of our soul.

But we can learn. We don't have to swap tomorrow's blessings for today's desires. Today, when nonfood hunger hunts us down and growls for satiation, we can recognize that hunger and ask, instead, for God to show us how to feed that pang with the only love that fills and endures.

TRAVELING MERCY

Dear one,
Hunger is a gift—
Hunger for me,
Hunger for life,
Hunger for meaning.
Use your hunger to your own advantage,
But do not use another's hunger
For your own advantage.
My plans are much larger
Than a cup of red lentils,
And you are worth far more
Than a bowl of stew.

NOTE TO SELF

Don't trade tomorrow for today.

Katie

APPETITE AS BIRTHRIGHT

Esau came in from the open country, famished.

—GENESIS 25:29

Perhaps we are more like Esau than Jacob. After all, we live in a society that over-utilizes the word *yes* and under-employs the word *no*. We say yes to self-fulfillment, yes to our hunger's desires, yes to satiation, yes please, yes, yes, yes, ASAP. But how often do we say no to ourselves, to our wants? Esau convicts me. How seldom I say no to myself. I say yes to a movie at night, yes to a little more chocolate, yes to more coffee. I say yes to an endless parade of minor indulgences. Like a crow, I fill my nest with cheap, shiny baubles.

Rationalizing that doesn't help. So they are minor indulgences. I am not a spendthrift; I rarely spend money on myself or the house or even other people. We eat out a handful of times a year. No problem, I can deny myself bigger things. But if I had the money, would I say no? In that way, my means limit me. This inability to say no to small treats strikes me too much like Esau the hunter and his bowl of stew. Maybe I need to pay attention to the difference between appetite and hunger. Maybe a simple no to myself

Katie

about that second very small, practically invisible to the naked eye, dish of chocolate chips. Maybe that tiny no could train me in living spiritually.

Maybe we could switch out our yeses, as though talking to a child and trying to help the child say yes to a better possibility. Rather than yes to chocolate, what about yes to a short walk down the street (and back, since you have to return sometime)? Or yes to a favorite song that makes you dance with joy around the living room for three minutes? Or no to a movie, yes to a novel or a favorite writer who deepens your experience of life and God.

But this is larger than myself. This yes-no issue is not only about myself and my own benefits: If I say yes to myself in unfulfilling or harmful or even unnecessary ways, I also say no to others. When I don't say yes to actively loving or serving someone, in reality I'm saying no. My lifestyle—private author, public speaker—keeps me in my office on weekdays and on a circuit most weekends. Deadlines, administrative tasks, and exhaustion have kept my hand down when people ask for volunteers and my head down to opportunities to serve.

Thousands of people die of hunger each week. Indulging our hunger pains—or discomfort, or wistfulness, or however hunger manifests itself—is not a birthright. It is not one of the benefits we receive for paying our dues in this world. Our privileged society dupes us into believing that life owes us something. Perhaps, rather, we owe life. And the occasional, or even frequent, no to myself allows me to say yes to life—life in this world. Yes to a life of loving other people.

Today, I'm going to practice with something simple. No to more chocolate and yes to . . . sweet words to the people in my life. And, here's another morsel: yes to the words that are "sweeter than honey, than honey from the honeycomb" (Ps. 19:10).

TRAVELING MERCY
Dear one,
A tiny no
Leads to a bigger yes—
To others,
To me,
And even to yourself.
Yes to loving more.
Yes to serving more.
Yes to really living
The sweet life.

NOTE TO SELF
Where do I say a small no, so I can say a bigger yes?

FOOD, FAST

"Look, I am about to die!"
—Genesis 25:32

Esau could write a bestselling book on deferred gratification. Or rather, he could write a book on the costs of not deferring gratification. His stomach began to rumble out in the countryside, and since apparently he hadn't thought to pack himself a lunch, he raced back home. Before he even reached the tents, the scent of hearty, simmering food wafted toward him. He tore in from the field and found Jacob quietly stirring a rich stew over the open fire.

Common sense capitulated to gnarling hunger, and Esau threw himself at his twin brother. "You have to feed me. I'm about to die!"

Jacob, calm as all get-out, looked at him without a blink. "First, sell me your birthright."

"What good is a birthright if I'm dead?" Esau asked. He probably had his funeral suit all pressed and ready to wear. Drooling with drama, he traded his entire birthright for a bowl of stew.

A bowl of stew. A few cups of beans.

For a birthright. It seems fair. If you're Jacob.

But Esau had one thing right: What good is a birthright if he's dying? It's irrelevant what you leave behind when you die. You can't, of course, take your riches with you. But must we hunger so much for today that we end up forfeiting tomorrow?

Even so, hunger is all-consuming—it eats its way through our natural boundaries of reason and practicality and insists on satisfaction. Now. We become demanding toddlers, ruled by our hunger.

Some people wonder if it's our inner tyrant taking over, demanding that our worth be validated by immediate treats, whether it's a stop at the refrigerator or the outlet mall, or a long romp on Facebook. Feed me, so I know I'm special, so I know I exist. Maybe that's part of the syndrome. But perhaps fear is at the root of the instant gratification society of today. Fear that we won't be OK, fear that acknowledges that tomorrow isn't guaranteed after all.

And even though we know better, even though we are probably schooled in the "Payday Someday" approach to living on earth while waiting for heaven, we still buy into the gotta-have-it-now mentality of this world. All those advertising bucks are rarely wasted on us.

If our birthright, like the birthright for Esau (or Jacob), is the privilege of inheritance for the blessing of helping our family and others navigate this world well—how much of that privilege do we exchange for today's version of the bowl of stew? Esau's birthright didn't just secure his own tomorrow. It secured the tomorrows of all the people he loved and would assume responsibility for.

Abraham's promise, passed down to Isaac and then to Jacob and Esau, was never intended for one man and his wife and child. It was intended for the world. We'd trade that on the market just to indulge our own internal, psychic hunger? That's the sadness in this story, and ours as well. Our own hunger and our own attempts to satisfy it don't just hurt us. They damage the people we love and people we don't even know yet.

How do we make sure we aren't caught or surprised by our hunger, or tempted to gratify it in self-defeating or other-harming ways? What if we instead learn to cook, learn to pack our own lunch, and learn to feed our souls in significant ways?

Then, because we've filled ourselves with the hearty stew of God's Word rather than proceed out of our emptiness and hunger (which leads us to do stupid things), we operate out of God's fullness.

TRAVELING MERCY
Dear one,
Food in the wilderness
Is sometimes scarce,
And hunger is frightening,
But know the difference
Between appetite and hunger,
Between drama and true need.
And you'll find
You have everything
Your heart desires
Just in time.

NOTE TO SELF
Function out of God's fullness.

FREEDOM

"I'm dying!"

—GENESIS 25:32 NLT

Esau inhaled the stew's fragrant aroma and gasped, practically in the throes of death. "I'm dying," he said. True enough, though he wasn't starving to death at that point. But aren't we all dying? Death, the great inevitable. But we can't die too soon. We must keep living until we die, and not stop living before we are dead. That's a challenge, with all the difficulties in this world, to stay alive and kicking, to keep living even with death as a guarantee. We don't always know how to live in the midst of dying.

Sometimes we kick the bucket long before anything kills us. Like Esau, who stopped living toward his future. We live dead. Dead of joy, dead of hope, dead of laughter. We live dead of compassion or an interest in others. We live cold as a cadaver, as though they've already injected formaldehyde into our veins and drained us of life's warm promise and presence.

Sometimes it is life's fault—blame a broken world with broken people for our deadness of spirit. Perhaps life is so painful that getting out of bed, whether emotionally or physically, hurts too much to be worth the investment. Perhaps you've been hurt badly, by people who were supposed to love and protect you.

Maybe, like Esau experienced, people take advantage of your weakness, of your frailty of spirit. The Jacobs in your life capitalize on your pain to their gain. And even if Jacob were simply being a shrewd leader, even if he were simply living out the prophecy God gave him (and he was, of course, though hurtful means), even if he wasn't taking advantage of a weaker brother but rather was walking forward in the best way he knew, Esau still lost out due to his own blindside, his appetite. It's as self-defeating as kicking the bucket with the bucket still full.

Undoubtedly his parents loved him, in their own unique ways. That's a plus. And, birthright or no, his life was still his own. In spite of Jacob's deal-making, Esau could still make the most of his life. He had much to live for.

But when we think we're dying, it's hard to keep living. Hard not to be hardened by the loss of hope, by the abandonment we feel. Fear grips our souls in its vise and we cannot slip loose or wrench ourselves free.

Maybe we can learn, though: learn to die to our fear. Learn to die to the past, to the words that hurt us, whether yesterday or long ago. Learn to die to anger that hardened into bitterness, or resentment. To die to our temporary hungers.

This doesn't mean pretending that we've never been hurt, never felt abandoned, never felt, like Esau, as the unchosen. It means owning up to all the negatives of life—these are part of our reality. It also means refusing to let those experiences and feelings own us. We don't have to live dead. By refusing to allow the negatives to be our inheritance, we live.

Like Esau, who sometime after Jacob evacuated made a significant life choice, we too begin to live. We throw off the yoke of those who exploit us, who pirate our sense of self or our gifts and offerings. We begin to live free. May God give us the wisdom to recognize what leads us toward death, that we may die only to that and gain the ability to live.

Free, indeed.

TRAVELING MERCY
Dear one,
I raise the dead.
But don't you live dead
On purpose.
Live alive and live free
Of enslavement to the short term
Of slavery to others' actions
And the shackles of past hurts.
Live
Free of the yoke.
You can
Live.

NOTE TO SELF
No one else determines my internal freedom.
Only God, and me.

DAILY LIFE

"What good is a birthright if I'm dead?"

—Genesis 25:32 msg

Don't go to your own funeral too soon. Don't give up hope for tomorrow's blessings, as Esau did, when you haven't even seen all of today's. Don't stop living until you're dead. That seems a good life motto, one that I witness year after year in a dear friend.

She served in World War II, raised her children, and had a passel of grandchildren. She buried her husband when they were far too young to say good-bye. They were just beginning to live, to learn to dance together. When the grandchildren were in varying stages of growing up, a car accident nearly killed her, crushing one leg and breaking the other. At eighty-five, she could have said, "I'm quitting now. I'm done. I'm disappointed and brokenhearted. It's too hard to do the work to get stronger." Healing is exhausting and painful; she knew this after years in the medical field.

Instead, she looked ahead at the lives of her family. "I want to go with them to Rome. I want to see my granddaughter confirmed. I want to be part of these significant moments and family milestones." In spite of her fractured leg and near death by sepsis, she chose the work required for life. When cleared to bear weight, she walked daily and grew strong. Months later, she laughed and rattled through Italy on trains and buses and rental cars with her family, overjoyed at God's goodness.

Her next setback occurred before her grandchild's wedding. Again, she refused to die too soon. She had taught her grandkids to dance years earlier; now it was her turn to cut a rug. "I will dance at her wedding," she declared. And she did, there under a big open-air tent with live music and wildflower centerpieces.

The next health crisis, when my friend neared ninety years old, threatened to take her to heaven. But by then her granddaughter was expecting my friend's first great-grandchild. My friend's eyes brightened with the invigoration of hope, of a plan. She would rock that baby. She would hold that baby in her arms. She would tell him all the secrets of living that she'd learned over many decades. Maybe she could teach him to dance.

And she did. Now another baby has joined the family, and this great woman and great-grandmother continues to live fully every single day. Kids have married, graduated from college, earned advanced degrees, and she was present to cheer and bless. She walks a mile a day, cooks, visits with her children and grandkids, and rocks those babies every chance she gets. She stays alive in every way, refusing to die a minute before she is dead.

Unlike Esau, she refuses to trade tomorrow for today. She will live today so she can live tomorrow. And the next day.

And when Jesus takes her to heaven, she can say she has lived into her birthright, the right to live deeply every single day. To live with joy in spite of limitations.

Each day, she awakens and asks, "Why am I still alive?" And every day, she answers, "To live. To love."

There's a reason it's called "daily life."

TRAVELING MERCY
Dear one,
Live today.
Dance, rock, cook, laugh, eat,
Love today.
Don't give away tomorrow in fear,
But live today.
And then tomorrow
Becomes the next day.
You live,
Dance, rock, cook, laugh, eat,
And love.

NOTE TO SELF
Live till I die. What's stopping me?

SEEING GREEN

"Do not go down to Egypt."

—Genesis 26:2

"Now there was a famine in the land," Genesis 26:1 says. Hunger is a frightening experience when the semitrucks loaded with food aren't getting through the checkpoints. When there's no one to find food or no money to buy it. Hungry people become submissive to the hands that offer to feed them. They become, literally, slaves to their hunger. Because too long hungry equals too soon dead. And our desire to live trumps the reticence to be enslaved.

In an agrarian society, you didn't just skip down to the corner store and bag your groceries on credit. For Isaac to be responsible for his family meant he needed to grow the food to feed them. With hills scorched brown and no leaves on the trees, no fruit, no olives, and no wheat in the fields, desperation would soon replace any denial. After a while, or preferably sooner, before people were surely and literally dying of hunger, Isaac would need a plan.

Running to Egypt, to the rich land along the great river Nile, made sense. Go to the greens. And Isaac knew the family story;

he knew that his father and mother had fled the previous famine for Egypt. Even though that trip nearly proved disastrous for Isaac's family, and certainly altered the trajectory of their lives, still, the facts now pointed to a return to Egypt for Abraham's clan. Go where you can find food.

But God overruled the fact of famine. "Stay in this land." Do not run off to satisfy your hunger elsewhere, in a foreign country.

It's easier, even sensible from the usual human perspective, to bolt to a foreign country, no matter what type of hunger afflicts us. To wait out the hunger pains, especially with a family to provide for and livestock to feed, requires more faith than I could manufacture.

Like most events in our lives, although only in retrospect perhaps, God's direction makes sense. To leave would mean the dissolution of Abraham's people. In Egypt, the compact family of four would be absorbed into the teeming culture. To leave would mean a certain death of their identity as a called-out people, a people God called and blessed in order to bless the rest of world. But Isaac couldn't know that, not from his view of the famine-afflicted lands, with his family and livestock bleating loudly in his ears.

God's hand doesn't always appear to be the logical, commonsense route to blessing and satisfaction. For us and for Isaac and for all the people who trusted him to provide for them, the good news is that God is bigger than the facts of our lives, bigger than the bare trees and the baked earth. Isaac stayed in Canaan, living in Philistia where King Abimelek reigned, heeding God's direction and trusting God's promise. And though history again repeated itself—like Abraham, Isaac passed off his beautiful wife as his sister in order to save his own neck—God set even that aright by disclosing the secret before great harm occurred.

After Isaac and his family lived in Gerar for "a long time," his crops increased a hundredfold (see Gen. 26:8–12). God fed the foursome and all their flocks and herds, and they flourished.

Sometimes we leave the country to find food; sometimes we stay put and experience God's miraculous provision right where we live.

Isaac and his family dwelled in the land. Isaac trusted the God who promised, and God, as always, proved faithful.

May we have the faith to know when to go and when to stay, that we might see God's faithfulness and live in God's provision. To look, like Isaac, beyond the facts to the faithfulness of God.

TRAVELING MERCY
Dear one,
What's your Egypt,
Your favorite go-to foreign country?
Where do you flee,
Bolt,
Escape,
When faced with your own
Drought-stricken life and soul
And relationships?
Can you come to me
In that fear and panic and hunger
When all you see is brown here
And green there
And let me lead you?
I will feed you.

NOTE TO SELF
Green means go . . . to God.
So does red. And brown.

JULY 15

LIVE IN THE LAND

"Stay in this land for a while, and I will be
with you and will bless you."

—Genesis 26:3

Today I waited with my hunger. I stayed in the land for a while. I rarely fast, at least, not deliberately, and I also rarely feel hunger pains because food options surround me. While I've lived in a few moments when I literally had nothing to eat and no money to buy food, those were rare and brief. Even though dieticians suggest that it's good to feel slightly hungry, to not feel full after every meal, hunger isn't one of my favorite experiences.

So today, I waited and allowed myself to actually feel hungry. Without instant satisfaction, hunger became the dominant note in the chord progression of the day. My stomach reminded me at ever-diminishing intervals, "Feed me. This is what you do. You are supposed to feed me. You have to feed the machine or the machine burns up." The hunger chorus became a pounding drum, which then consumed my focus. "I'm hungry. What should I eat? What sounds good?" Soon it was both the chorus and the entire song. The orange marmalade that I would never eat given other options, the can of beets that has sat in the pantry for four years, the stale chips crushed in the bottom of the snack pile—all of these acquire a new lure in the midst of hunger.

While I listened to and tried to pray through the internal growling, I began to realize that sometimes my hunger is about wanting comfort. It's due to fear of the unknown or to stresses I can't control. Or maybe it's a happy snack to celebrate good news or a reward for hard work. Or it's an escape from tedium, from work that I don't like or don't feel like doing. Eating for avoidance! Too often, the hunger is more emotional longing than physical necessity.

Perhaps this is part of the thinking behind the discipline of fasting: that every time we feel hunger, we move to God in prayer. We remove ourselves and our hunger from our focal point, and look beyond. We notice our own hunger-needs and direct those longings to God. We pray for people around the world who are hungry. For the people who grow and harvest the crops we eat, so many workers underpaid or exploited. We pray for the agencies that raise funds and organize so that children and adults do not die of hunger or malnourishment. We invite God to show us how to help people who are hungry, hungry for food or love or safety or hope. We pray. With every hunger pain, we refocus our concentration. We notice hunger pains, and our pain takes us to God. We become people who, rather than being owned by our hunger, own the hunger, which then becomes a vehicle for prayer.

We eat too soon; we spoil our appetite. Our appetite for what? For God. For being an instrument in this world that effects change. People whose needs are consistently met are in danger of complacency. Hunger, properly harnessed, can become a force for good.

Isaac's hunger pushed him to God, and in his hunger, he heard anew the generation-old promise, "I will be with you and bless you." Trust me, God said. Trust me through the hunger, and watch how I feed you; watch how I bless.

TRAVELING MERCY
Dear one,
You are hungry
For so many things.
But stay in the land a while;
Harness your hunger.
Let it bring you to my heart,
And yours,
And my heart for the hungry in this world,
Those hungry for love,
Nurture, direction, meaning, safety,
And, yes, for food.
What are you hungry for?

NOTE TO SELF
Wait until hunger becomes a spiritual discipline.

DIGGING DEEP

From there he went up to Beersheba. That night
the Lord appeared to him.

—Genesis 26:23–24

Isaac created space for God to act; God gave him room;
and for Isaac's next act he headed up to Beersheba, meaning
the "well of the oath" or "seven wells." He hauled off to a place
legendary in his family's lore. Surely as he walked, he replayed
family history.

Into the desert of Beersheba, where Abraham long ago
sent Hagar and Ishmael, after Isaac's fateful birthday party,
and split the family. Later in Beersheba, Abimelek recognized
God's presence with Abraham: "God is with you in everything
you do." There the two leaders swore an oath and honored
Abraham's digging of a well. There the patriarch planted a
tamarisk tree, and there, the Scriptures tell us, "he called on
the name of the Lord, the Eternal God" (Gen. 21:33).

After the aged Abraham hiked to the region of Moriah
with his son Isaac, after God delivered them both from that
sacrifice, Abraham returned to Beersheba with his servants.
(Isaac's name is notably missing from that return journey's
record.)

And now Isaac added a fresh layer—he, like his father, passed his wife off as his sister (Gen. 26:7–11).

So Beersheba became an area of both provision and desertion. To Beersheba Isaac went, our first record of his travels to the area. How difficult this must have been, yet another walk by faith in a lifetime of walking by faith, a lifetime of trying to live beyond the wounds rather than be bound by them.

He returned to the land that reminded him of abandonment, of failure. Yet, that night, because Isaac created space, he heard for the first time God's promise to him, personally. Until then he'd possessed hand-me-down knowledge, stories told around many campfires as sparks flew into the night sky, stories of God calling his father, God promising his papa blessing and greatness and an entire nation of descendants.

But this night, after Isaac trusted God and moved ahead with his life rather than getting stuck by quarrels and his own possibly legitimate rights to the wells he'd opened, after he dug deep and struck water, Isaac headed to a place of family familiarity. Isaac created space for God to act, and act God did. God spoke.

In power and personally, God reiterated the promise made decades before. "I am the God of your father Abraham," God said. "Do not be afraid, for I am with you; I will bless you and will increase the number of your descendants for the sake of my servant Abraham."

Listen to that assurance: "Do not be afraid, for I am with you." Do not be afraid, God says to us, just as to Isaac so long ago. "I am with you." With me, with you, with us. Miracle of miracles, we need not fear the lack of water or the quarrels over wells, we need not fear the past or the weight of our wounds, because God is with us. We can revisit territory from our past, with its family traffic patterns that left cross-hatches of pain, and know the truth just as Isaac knew: "Do not be afraid, for I am with you."

But the promise continues from there. God will bless, God will increase our descendants, and God will give us a legacy in this land to which we're called. God will. God promised Isaac, in honor of Abraham, and we, too, are Abraham's offspring. "If you belong to Christ, then you are Abraham's seed, and heirs according to the promise" (Gal. 3:29).

That night, after hearing God's voice for the first time, Isaac built an altar to the Lord. To worship this God who provides.

Water in the desert, yes. Relief from fear, yes. Freedom from our past, yes.

Yes, yes, yes. We build an altar on the stones of God's presence and promise, an altar of worship, smack-dab in the middle of our nighttime. Worship in the desert.

TRAVELING MERCY

Dear one,
What's true for Isaac
Is true for you.
Do not be afraid,
For I am with you.
Yesterday's wounds,
Today's dryness,
Tomorrow's fruitfulness.
I am with you.
So do not be afraid,
But rather
Make like Isaac
And build an altar
Out of the stones of praise.

NOTE TO SELF

Wounds or wells . . . God is with me.

NO FEAR . . . WHY?

"Do not be afraid, for I am with you."

—Genesis 26:24

"Do not be afraid," God told Isaac, there in the desert with the question of water rights unresolved. Isaac survived the famine and flourished, but would not live long without access to a well.

"Don't be afraid." But we are. We are afraid. We are, too often, very afraid, and sometimes fear is warranted. Sometimes, maybe often, it isn't. When fear abscesses in our souls, fear wins. A daily diet of fear will destroy our internal organs and corrode our psyche. It hurts relationships. It distracts us. It renders us impotent against life's natural challenges and can lead us down the dismal path to depression and discouragement.

Whether we're afraid of trigonometry tests, failure, death, public speaking, falling, heights, water, fire, spiders, snakes, centipedes, or terrorists, excessive fear stinks. Granted, fear can sometimes save our lives, but more often than not, fear ends up a reaction to triggers that are not life threatening. Comfort threatening, perhaps, or status threatening.

Even so, the word *fear* appears hundreds of times in the Scriptures, and the phrase "Do not be afraid" seventy times.

So fear is relevant to us or it wouldn't be a frequent mention in the Bible.

"Do not be afraid," however, is a platitude. It is a powerless order, an empty phrase. Unless . . . unless the one uttering the phrase—or command—can back it up with power.

I'm guessing that's the case with God. God puts muscle to the command with a resounding reason. In every Genesis instance when God uses the phrase "Do not be afraid," it is then backed up with God's might, presence, protection, and guidance. After Abram rescued Lot in Genesis 14, Abram's lack of an heir occupied all his soul-space. Into that fearful spot, God appeared in a vision and said, "Do not be afraid, Abram. I am your shield, your very great reward" (Gen. 15:1). God the protector. God the reward. God the I AM.

In Genesis 21:17–18, Hagar landed in the wilderness, homeless and hungry with a child to sustain. The angel of the Lord appeared and said, "Do not be afraid; God has heard the boy crying as he lies there. Lift the boy up and take him by the hand, for I will make him into a great nation." God would provide the muscle behind the promise.

Fast forward to Isaac, years later, post-famine. "Do not be afraid, for I am with you" (Gen. 26:24). Don't be afraid, because . . . why? Because God was with him. And again to Jacob, years down the road, "Do not be afraid to go down to Egypt, for I will make you into a great nation there" (Gen. 46:3).

Do not be afraid. Because why, again?

Because I AM. Because I, God, the I AM, am with you. Because God flexes the biceps of heaven with the command, "Do not be afraid."

So today, when my own fear rises up, I hear God's words again and again: "Do not be afraid." This time, though, I listen. My heart rate slows and the panicked bird inside my rib cage lights, tucking its wings tight.

Why? Because God.

TRAVELING MERCY

Dear one,
Of course you will fear.
But do not allow the fear
To distance you from the truth.
My truth.
I Am.
I am the God of Abraham
Of Isaac
Of Jacob
Of you.
"Do not be afraid"
Becomes a promise of my protection
My provision
My power.
I Am,
And you are not;
But that's OK.
So hear my words
One more time.
Do
Not
Fear.
Because I Am.

NOTE TO SELF

God is. I am not. That's good.

OPENING WELLS

There he pitched his tent, and there his servants dug a well.
—GENESIS 26:25

One leg of Isaac's journey included reopening wells that his father had dug years before. But contention surrounded every well he opened, as local herders fought for ownership so they could water their livestock. So Isaac shifted and dug new wells (also all hotly contested).

Without water, people perished. The critical element of water meant territorial battles and fights for water rights.

Isaac understood the land and that water sometimes exists in the most unlikely and inhospitable of situations. But Isaac's certainty extended beyond the belief that water waited beneath the surface of the land. He knew the God who provided water.

After one well-fight too many, Isaac "moved on . . . and dug another well, and no one quarreled over it. He named it Rehoboth, saying, 'Now the LORD has given us room and we will flourish in the land'" (see Gen. 26:17–22). Rather than fight, he moved his life forward.

He hiked onward until he found an uncontested water source, and there dug a well. Deep in the core of his soul, he surely knew that the God who provided for him so many years ago would provide for him now. Isaac trusted God for living space and for what he needed to live well, and God provided. We see faith in the naming of this place, for *Rehoboth* means "room."

Moving on requires wisdom and faith. Leaving behind the quarrels and stepping out into new, uncontested territory forced Isaac to live what he believed, the lesson he'd learned on a bundle of kindling with a knife poised one trembling inch from his throat. Strapped to that altar, he'd discovered firsthand that God provides, that God is faithful.

Isaac put that major life lesson to good use as he hiked farther in the land of Only God Knows Where. And when he struck water, with uncontested water rights, his response? "There he pitched his tent, and there his servants dug a well" (Gen. 26:25). Isaac pounded down stakes and praised the Lord for room to live.

So many of us live like human trash compactors, cramming more duties and events and people into the small compartments of our lives and souls, everything jammed into our limited waking hours. We pound and push and wedge more into our lives, and steal from the night to complete or at least attack our long list of obligations. But the Lord gives us room, even if we don't recognize our need for space or even the wisdom of space. Wisdom and faith demand that we seek the soul space we require, that we recognize our need for room to flourish. No one can do this for us.

Whether emotional room, psychological room, or physical space, the Lord has given us room.

Space means the potential to flourish, to expand. "The Lord has given us room," Isaac said. "We will flourish in the land." We, too, can find refuge in the God who provides room—we can seek out soul space, breathing room, where we rest in God's presence and provision. There, like Isaac, we can flourish.

TRAVELING MERCY
Dear one,
People will fight over life-giving
Water
And look for life in the fight
Rather than look for a new well.
Don't fight.
Walk forward.
Live in the middle of my presence
And I will provide for you.
They don't call me
"God will provide"
For nothing.

NOTE TO SELF
Don't fight. Move forward.
There's more where that came from.

A LIFE AND DEATH GUIDE

He called for Esau his older son. . . . "I am now an
old man and don't know the day of my death."

—GENESIS 27:1–2

Losing his eyesight, feeling his years. Though he was
probably only around a hundred years old, it was time. Time
for Isaac to bestow the blessing on his elder son in order to
transfer the clan's leadership and the responsibility for the
estate to the next generation. Legally binding, the blessing
proclaimed the son's destiny as the next leader.

He called in his son, Esau, to prepare him for the ceremony.
"I am now an old man," he said, "and don't know the day of my
death."

Join the crowd, Isaac. None of us know the day of our death,
and similarly, few of us prepare very well for its inevitability.
I laugh at bragging statistics, "Death rate lower . . ." Last I
checked, the only way out was death. It's a 100 percent, all-in,
guarantee. No one escapes the confines of earth's tenure without
death, Enoch being one notable exception. (The Scriptures
tell us, "Enoch walked faithfully with God; then he was no
more, because God took him away" [Gen. 5:24].) Only a
handful of people in the record book get out without dying.

So ignoring the eventual fact of death doesn't make it disappear. Isaac paid attention and planned ahead. That puts him in the top percentile of forward thinkers.

Wise people consider the future, as Isaac did when he called in his elder son. Though death would reach him many years later, Isaac beat that last-minute panic by arranging the blessing for his boy.

"I don't know the day of my death," he said. Only God knows that date for any of us, but thankfully, God knows. We needn't live anxiously, wondering about that day, but being ready seems a good idea. How many of us fail to plan on the likelihood of death? Not just in making a will, but in inviting people into significant discussions about their futures, our future, and our hope of heaven. Isaac planned ahead by preparing to bless his firstborn son (however underhanded that entire scenario played out).

Like Isaac, we don't know the day of our death, nor that of others. We've all been surprised by others' untimely (at least on our timelines) deaths, as were their families.

More than surprised, we're often filled with regret. If only we'd loved them more, forgiven them sooner, been with them more, called or wrote them more, or helped more. If only we hadn't been impatient, shirked intimacy, or been unavailable or fearful. Why didn't we return that last call, answer that letter, stop to talk to the neighbor at the mailbox one last time, offered a hand or some hope? We all can fill in those blanks; we can name people whose deaths filled us with loss and left us shaking our heads at ourselves for not acting sooner or more often.

If we knew today that it would be our last, how would we live? How would we bless? How would we love? How would we live differently today than we lived yesterday?

Death, after all, is no respecter of age. Young or old, no matter our age, we owe it to ourselves and to others to figure out, before we breathe our last, how we will live today. How we will love today. Serve today. Give today. Bless today.

Sort of a new take on a living will.

TRAVELING MERCY
Dear one,
Plan ahead;
Prepare to bless;
Learn to love;
Live without regrets.
No one knows the day of death
But I do.
Today, however,
Decide—
How will you love?

NOTE TO SELF
In loving others I die to myself.

THE SCOREKEEPER

He called for Esau his older son.

—GENESIS 27:1

After the famine and the digging of wells, the twins turn forty, and Isaac turns the corner on a century of living. So far, Jacob and Esau tied the score in terms of integrity. Or not. Jacob connived for Esau's birthright, and Esau's appetite ruled him to the point of total disregard for the gift he tossed away. Neither twin ranks high on the conscience-meter.

Kids aren't born into a vacuum, and between nature and nurture a lot of, or at least some, behavior can be explained. So the next scene with our battle-scarred patriarch, Isaac, reveals a great deal.

According to the cultural context, giving the blessing required witnesses in order to render it a legal ceremony and transaction. Isaac called Esau in on the sly and told no one else about the upcoming rite. Why keep it a secret? Isn't it possible that Isaac knew God's prophecy to Rebekah, of the younger son ruling the elder? Isn't it possible, since we know from the Scriptures that Isaac favored Esau (see Gen. 25:28), that this father simply wanted his own personal favorite in the role of leadership?

Isaac had a taste for wild game, and Esau was a skilled hunter. Of course they got along well. So is this like father, like son? Because evidently Isaac's appetite got the best of him, too, as he sent Esau off to hunt down and prepare his favorite meal. Rebekah, who'd pressed her ear to the tent to hear what her husband told Esau, took advantage of Esau's foray into the field for game. She prepared Isaac's favorite meal then hustled Jacob into his costume.

None seemed overly concerned with keeping a clean ledger in their moral books. But cast too fine a net and you may end up catching yourself. When Jacob appeared, smelling and feeling like Esau but speaking with Jacob's voice, Isaac knew the difference. Why didn't he stop the charade? But how could he? He was holding a secret ceremony, and to blow the whistle blew his own cover. And of course Jacob's cover.

In spite of the trickery, the story leads things where God intended. Were there scrupulous ways to achieve that? Absolutely. But in spite of knowing right and wrong, we humans walk a hobbledy line. What a miracle that God's work ever gets done on earth when we are often the means of its accomplishment; what a miracle to be part of the storyline, though we rarely, if ever, appear as shining stars.

Without conflict, we'd have a dull, unrelatable, and unrealistic tale in the family line of Abraham, Isaac, and Jacob. Without flawed characters, the saga becomes a fairy tale or a myth. Without normal petty likes and dislikes, without overwhelming appetites and cunning lead roles, we have no story. We have no miracle. We have no need of the God who promised to make us all a blessing. Plus, it's so boring.

Not only do we see ourselves in this story of self-centeredness and deviousness, we also get to see God, the God who promised. The God who delivered. The God who has never stopped inviting us into heaven's story, even with our flawed characters and conflicted values.

Score? God wins. And then invites us to be on the team. Now that's a miracle.

TRAVELING MERCY

Dear one,
We are on the same team,
But one of us has
An advantage.
I can see how it all fits together
In spite of the broken people
Playing on the field.
Conflict since Eden;
Cunning since the first garden.
I know.
I see.
And I am waiting
For the day
When we all live
In one accord,
Working together,
Laughing together,
Helping one another
Play fair.

NOTE TO SELF

Talk first, act second.
Communication avoids conflict.

THE CONSCIENCE CALL

"Now, my son, listen carefully and do what I tell you."

—GENESIS 27:8

Significant power accompanied the blessing, a conferring of financial status and authority at sacrificial meals, burial matters, and the role of kinsman-redeemer. Getting wind of the upcoming blessing ceremony, Rebekah secreted Jacob away: "Quick, shoot the game your father loves. I'll prepare it just the way he likes it, disguising you like Esau. Then *you* get the blessing." Jacob cooperated, put sheepskin on his bare flesh and wool on his hands and arms, and dressed up in Esau's field-scented clothing. It's easy to overlook Jacob's immediate response.

Though Jacob ended up with the birthright after Esau's hunger captured Jacob's conscience, Jacob's response to his mother's bright blessing idea glimmers of a deeper well of integrity. He protests, however weakly: "I would appear to be tricking him and would bring down a curse on myself rather than a blessing" (Gen. 27:12). Jacob knew their stories and heritage. Abraham's people were meant to be a blessing to others. To bless and serve in life-giving ways seems to be the opposite of taking care of your own business. Jacob's reaction here does him credit.

His mother prevailed with a drastic vow. "My son, let the curse fall on me. Just do what I say; go and get them for me" (Gen. 27:13).

God prophesied and likely planned to implement Jacob's leadership. But how could Rebekah know this? Her only recorded personal interchange with God occurred at that moment in her pregnancy, at least forty years earlier. While I don't blame her for *wanting* to help fulfill that prophecy (if her favoritism and dishonest plan even slightly included that motive), how much of that desire grew from spiritual devotion versus wanting her favorite son to have the favored blessing?

Jacob would rule over Esau, but Rebekah's determination to force it by trickery tore apart her family, reigniting a civil war between her sons.

Securing blessing by deceit is entirely at odds with God's calling to Abraham to bless others. Were there ways to get that blessing conferred on Jacob without the treachery? Yes. It's called communication, with God and with the people involved.

I mourn the loss of the delightful, serving, loving Rebekah of sixty years prior at the well in Harran. I'd love to believe that Rebekah had God's prophecy about her sons at the forefront of her mind, but because of rustic communication skills and the underprivileged status of women in that culture, she felt the only way to bring it to pass was by this damaging masquerade.

God delivered on the prophecy. But the journey to fulfillment seems far less miraculous by the disconcerting effort on the part of Rebekah and Jacob to secure that blessing.

But who consistently demonstrates pure motives? How often do I pray and think, simultaneously, how beautiful that prayer's phrasing, or hope I remember what I said so I can write it down after I open my eyes? Or how often do I serve another entirely out of love, without any hopes for reciprocity or personal advancement?

Maybe that's what we glean from our encounter with Rebekah: a wholly human woman, with a parent's fierce but flawed love. We admire her love, grieve her scheming desperation. And pray that we notice our own flawed loving, inviting God to bless through us in ways that make God look good.

God's purposes will be accomplished in this world, with or without us. But how much more fun if they're achieved with and through us?

TRAVELING MERCY

Dear one,
Hold tight to the promise.
It extends throughout the ages—
Through Abraham,
Isaac,
And, yes,
Rebekah, too.
And through you.
There is no expiration date
On my promise
Or my faithfulness.
Let's work together
To bring the reign
To earth.

NOTE TO SELF

Build into blessing by cooperation.

FAMILY FLAWS

"Let the curse fall on me."

—Genesis 27:13

Rebekah's dogged determination and deceit to bring her favorite son into receipt of the blessing surely robbed her marriage of trust. Isaac must have already suffered from some abandonment issues, after carrying his own wood for his funeral pyre and laying himself down upon it for his father to sacrifice.

Add, then, the sense of betrayal and powerlessness that resulted from his wife's actions. She eavesdropped on Isaac's conversation with Esau, abandoned her vow to her husband, played him for a fool, and took advantage of his disability. That level of disloyalty surely dug a deep ravine between the couple and further fractured Isaac's heart and soul. It probably didn't help Rebekah live with a clean conscience, either.

Might it have been easier to clue Isaac in on God's words to her and consider together how they might bring the prophecy to pass without such damage? For, though she said, "let the curse be upon me," the fallout from her actions hurt the entire family. Isaac's anger seems clear enough: "Your brother came deceitfully and took your blessing" (Gen. 27:35).

Add to that the damage to his marriage, and to his soul, abandoned yet again. Plus, Isaac fiddled with deceit in securing the blessing for Esau without the necessary legal proceedings. So his own sin piled onto the already ample possibilities for pain.

And then the cost to Esau, who followed his father's instructions for the blessing honestly: He not only lost the blessing, but also his ties with his mother and brother. Esau and Jacob's relationship immediately fractured, with Esau uttering threats to kill him as soon as their father died and the mourning period ended. With that danger haunting him, Jacob escaped from the family and sought asylum with an uncle who would treat him less than honorably, as an indentured servant.

Be careful what you wish for, we should whisper to Rebekah. The fallout from her formidable choice indeed resulted in a curse upon her. She would not live to see her favorite son again— she is never again mentioned in the account of Isaac's life. No one highlights Rebekah's death nor weeps at her graveside. In fact, in Genesis 35:8 we learn that Deborah, Rebekah's nurse, died, but we never hear about Rebekah's death. All that we know for certain about her is that Isaac and Rebekah were buried in the same place, alongside the bones of Abraham and Sarah (see Gen. 49:31).

Perhaps Rebekah lived long enough to wonder if the fallout from her trickery could have been avoided and the goal accomplished some other way.

As it was, Jacob's heritage resulted in a figurative and emotional disinheritance for Rebekah. A sorrow like a thorn in her heart pricked the rest of her days, a forlorn mother standing at the edge of the family tents, hands shielding her eyes from the sun's glare that she might glimpse her son's return. She waited in vain.

This, however, is the miracle: that in a family where all four members share guilt in the family dysfunction, this family is the single family God chose to carry forward the charge, promise, and responsibility of Abraham. This flawed family?

Yes. Just like yours. Just like mine. There is, after all, hope. What do we say to that?

Forward.

TRAVELING MERCY

Dear one,
Broken people are part
Of my master plan.
There are no other types
On this earth.
Only in heaven are you
Unbroken.
Flawed people
Form the foundation
Of all the work in this world.
So don't stop working,
But lean into healing
As you put your shoulder to the task
And move forward.
Together.

NOTE TO SELF

Flawed people—like me!—always lead the front line.

A LISTENING EAR

"The voice is the voice of Jacob."

—Genesis 27:22

Did Isaac regret not listening to his screaming inner sense that said, "This is not your son Esau. This is Jacob"? How long did his self-recriminations last; how long did the tension ripen and the rift increase between him and Rebekah? How long would he hold on to the fallout of yet another betrayal in his life, of yet another example of abandonment? Because surely those feelings swarmed over and around him like a hive of bees when he realized he was trapped in his and his wife's trickery. Surely when Esau came and wept for a blessing, Isaac's heart broke and the shaking finger of shame began waving.

Hopefully, God opened the eyes of Isaac's heart to see the truth. God works with the tools on the table—which would be all of us wounded and deceiving and scheming and hoping people—and brings about the future. Isaac's handing off the blessing to the wrong son ended up being the way God got the work moving forward, the work of being a blessing in this world, the means of establishing the people who would multiply and spread and ultimately bring the promised Savior of the world.

Isn't it so in our own lives, as well? We shame ourselves, telling our poor inner soul that we are worthless, that no one else would have acted that way, that if we were worth a grain of salt or had an ounce of sense we'd have listened to the screaming difference in voices and gone with our gut. Or we let another's deception nibble and gnaw its way through our most vital relationships. Or we give in to bitterness and regret. However this scenario plays out, all possible endings reveal our own duplicity.

Eventually, though, to arrive at peace, we park on the salient truth seen in these stories: In spite of the lies and disguises, in spite of deceit and desertion, in spite of every single thing wrong with life on earth and relationships on this planet, God has a plan. God's plan is for good, and God the great recycler will take the deplorable situations and still bring about that plan.

It's what God does.

Meanwhile, in situations where we are caught between the unknown and the not-quite-right, we can cultivate the ability to listen deeply. To hear the disquiet as a sign to listen, and begin to ask, "What does this mean?" To listen to that intuition, to the sixth sense, or to the quiet voice of the Holy Spirit. Jesus would say, years later, using yet another gamey image Isaac and Esau and Jacob would surely have understood, "His sheep follow him because they know his voice" (John 10:4).

There is, after all, no good reason to second-guess our past unless we learn from it, unless we grow into people of greater faith in God and greater repentance for our own awfulness, our not-listening, or our failure to believe the voice we hear. May we learn to listen to the voice within and grow to trust that God's outcome is always for good. No matter the mistakes and challenges of the in-between.

TRAVELING MERCY

Dear one,
Hear me on this.
Listen up,
Because
The more you listen,
The more you will live,
The better you will live,
And the longer you will live
Without shame and blame
And the what-if game
Which no one wins.
So stop to listen
To my voice,
And the more you listen,
The more you will recognize
And follow me.
And together we'll add more branches
To the family tree.
From Abraham to Isaac to Jacob
All the way through
To thee.

NOTE TO SELF

Listen honestly and act from that center.

FOR WANT OF A BLESSING

"Do you have only one blessing, my father?
Bless me too, my father!"

—GENESIS 27:38

When Esau learned that the blessing of the firstborn landed on his younger brother's head, his voice cracked and his heartbreak spilled out. "Do you have only one blessing, my father? Bless me too," he cried. His father, too, when faced with the truth, that the blessing fell on Jacob instead of Esau, "trembled violently" (Gen. 27:33).

The longing for blessing speaks of a deep soul-ache, a wound felt by men and women around the world. The blessing of parents over children, a proclamation of God's provision for them and faithfulness to them, pours over all the broken places of our souls and mortars in the cracks.

In a world where parents' presence or lack of presence plays an enormous role in their children's success or failure, we hear Esau's cry as doubly relevant. Perhaps even in your own life, the longing for a parent's blessing still leaves a panging hollowness inside. To live without blessing is to live, in some ways, unfulfilled, or at least uncertain. Without the affirmation of blessing, without someone calling out our gifts and our creativities, without someone carrying their dreams and their hopes for our futures to God, we live with only a partial and wobbly foundation.

Throughout our years, we can be aware of that lack of foundation, but it needn't determine negatively how we live our lives. Forming strong relationships with people who see our gifts, who invite us into fulfillment of them, gives a resiliency to resist the natural decay that comes from lack of affirmation.

So keep track of those people who affirm your gifts, who call out your innate strengths. Make it a priority to surround yourself with people who walk in their gifts and callings with integrity and who grow through challenges. Even if your parents haven't blessed you in ways that you can recognize, even if your past left fissures in your soul's foundation, the final word hasn't been spoken by those lacks. Rather, the real blessing comes from the words of God over us, from the certainty that God loves us and calls us and yes, blesses us from heaven. And through the people around us.

Esau's heart-rending words still echo through the generations, thousands of years later: "Do you have only one blessing, my father?"

The answer for us today? No. God is not limited to one blessing as Isaac was, one blessing to confirm on only one child. God adopts us into this great big family, calls us heirs, and promises blessing after blessing after blessing through time, from eternity, from the people around us, from heaven.

We can indeed cry with Esau, "Bless me, too! Bless me, too."

And God will, because God does. Bless and bless and bless. And we can rise up from our heartache and soul-break and life fractures, because God's word over us in Jeremiah 31:3 is true: "I have loved you with an everlasting love."

That's quite an inheritance.

TRAVELING MERCY

Dear one,
Others' voices ring and clang
So loudly
And their silences, too.
But hear this,
Listen up,
Listen well:
I've written my love on your heart,
And you can see it spreading
From horizon to horizon.
I've engraved your name
On the palm of my hand.
Hear me
Over all those other soul-wounds,
Over that longing for a blessing.
Let me bless you.
You are my beloved,
And I choose you.
Live, now, in that love.

NOTE TO SELF

Who surrounds me with blessing and calls out my gifts?

CONVERTING

"Only one blessing . . . ?"

—GENESIS 27:38

When Esau begged his father for a blessing, Isaac's first words were enough to shoot fire and ice through anyone's veins. Isaac combined a list of top dreads—"Your dwelling will be away from the earth's richness, away from the dew of heaven"—terrible words for a hunter and gatherer to hear (Gen. 27:40).

Hunters rely on the earth's richness, they depend on the dew of heaven, because otherwise, famine kills off their prey. Livelihoods dry up. People begin to die. So rather than a blessing, Isaac's words sound like a dismal dose of doomsday.

But he didn't stop there. "You will live by the sword," Isaac said. Not by the bow and arrow, which were likely standard hunting weaponry in those days. It was surely what Esau used to hunt the game for the blessing feast. But he would live "by the sword"—in other words, defending himself and fighting for his life, or fending off predators.

It's so far short of a blessing. Esau probably kept on weeping or ripped out some of his abundant hair by the handful.

But who is to say that what felt like a curse wasn't actually, in the course of a lifetime, a blessing? In fact, not only did Esau never deliver on his murderous threat, he appears later in the story as a man who was successful both in family life and in terms of his workaday world. He had everything he needed, "plenty," he told Jacob two decades after that fateful day (see Gen. 33:9).

It's entirely possible that what felt like a curse rather than a blessing, actually became the very means that brought Esau to the end of his irresponsibility and made a man of him. He discovered, it would seem, gifts and talents that he didn't know he possessed. An acumen that perhaps, had he been the one to rule the roost fiscally and spiritually, he might never have needed to encounter. Inclement weather is the mother of shelter, and Esau had plenty of inclement going on.

Isn't this so for us as well? The situations that seem to bow us, to deplete us of all hope; the events that nearly break us across the rim of despair; the people who wound us without a drop of compassion for the damage and havoc wreaked on our lives—properly tended, these all become avenues of bringing out our very best capabilities. Our wounds become the trail of discovery, our wreckage the jumbled puzzle pieces of creativity.

When faced with the worst life could hand him, Esau did not capitulate. When his fault line split, Esau eventually learned how to bridge the chasm. When his luck ran out, his fortitude appeared.

TRAVELING MERCY

Dear one,
I convert
Nonblessings
Into real blessings.
You and I
Together
Can bring good from the bad
Done to you,
Can wring function
From the dysfunction,
And hope
From the empty places.
Do not capitulate.
You and I
Will build a bridge
Clear into the future.

NOTE TO SELF

Fissures help invent bridges.

SEEING RED

"But when you grow restless, you will throw his
yoke from off your neck."

—Genesis 27:40

Many years pass before Isaac's blessing of Esau comes to
fruition—or at least, before we see that fruit. But while the
first two sentences seem more curse than blessing, the final
line holds the breath of hope: "But when you grow restless,
you will throw his yoke from off your neck."

While we wait for that moment when the throwing aside
of the yoke occurs, what, we ask, is the yoke? Throw his
yoke—the servitude in Genesis 27:40. "You will serve your
brother," Isaac said. Jacob would leave the family, escape
the death threats, prosper in the family home of his mother,
and return a rich man. The Scriptures don't show us a single
scene of Esau serving Jacob. Jacob is out of the picture for
many years, and there is no mention of servitude between
the twins.

So what bondage, what yoke, bound Esau to Jacob in
servitude? Where do we see a yoke of any kind?

What about his anger that turned to the need for revenge?
Anger over the stolen blessing. Anger that refused to be

relinquished. That anger converted into a murderous plot with Esau streaming threats about killing Jacob the thief.

Anger, unresolved, colors our vision with red, blood red. Anger activates the fight or flight reaction (so essential to hunters like Esau), dumps energy into the heart, and then pushes it through the body rapidly via a surge in heart rate and blood pressure. It puts on hold any bodily functions not immediately essential to fighting, functions like digestion and healing. The fight or flight reaction decreases circulation to non-fighting muscles.[1]

But too much anger, too frequent anger? Atherosclerosis accelerates, building up plaque in the arteries. The heart works harder, the vessels squeeze more often, and blood pressure increases. More glucose in the blood, more fat globules . . . and *voila!* Experts call this effect of anger "cardiotoxic": poisonous to the heart.[2]

Anger also functions as a great motivator. When people convert their anger to action, the energy surge fights against injustice, increases determination to set matters right, and supplies the energy to accomplish goals. But unconverted chronic anger poisons our hearts.

It doesn't do wonders for relationships, either. Anger hardens those as well as hearts. It can lead to not only murder, but a slow suicide of soul and eventually, perhaps, of our very lives.

So what underlies our anger? Sometimes our anger rises when we ask the questions, "Am I valuable? Do you love me? Do I have worth?" and hear the answer, "No. Absolutely not." Surely this answer fueled Esau's rage.

But anger also bubbles when we then ask, "Who is in charge here?" and fear answers: "No one is in charge. You are on your own. Your future is going to be a disaster and no one cares." That fear leads to anger at our sense of abandonment.

Perhaps both questions, "Do you love me?" and "Who's in charge here?" are rooted in fear of abandonment. Abandonment seems to confirm that we are on our own and that no one loves us, so it provides ready answers to all these questions before we even know we've asked them.

Seeing red? Tuning in to anger and asking, "What am I angry about here? How much of that anger is about abandonment or fear?" slows down our heart rate and our angry reaction. It forces us out of the flash-fire emotional side of our brain and into the rational, let's-think-this-through side. We can stop throwing word bombs or plates and stop dumping hormones into our bloodstream and decide how to respond to the situation.

Anger asks powerful and good questions. Our answers may well mean life or death.

TRAVELING MERCY

Dear one,
Anger is a tool
I gave you,
But a tool to build
Not to destroy.
Pay attention to your anger.
Use your anger
As impetus for good,
For positive change—
To right wrongs,
To fight for justice,
To flee from danger.
But not to hurt another.
If—when—you see red,
Turn your eyes to me.
I will help you to see
My way.
And remember—I always
Answer the question,
"Do you love me?" with,
"Yes."

NOTE TO SELF

Anger asks good questions. How do I answer?

NOTES

1. Danica Collins, "The Deadly Effects of Anger on Your Health and Mind," Underground Health Reporter, accessed June 23, 2014, http://undergroundhealthreporter.com/effects-of-anger-dangerous-to-health-and-mind/#axzz35UHGE2op.

2. Katherine Kam, "How Anger Hurts Your Heart," WebMD, accessed June 23, 2014, http://www.webmd.com/balance/stress-management/features/how-anger-hurts-your-heart.

THE WEEK OF LASTS

"Leave immediately for Paddan Aram!
Go to the house of Bethuel."

—Genesis 28:2 net

Rebekah, on high alert after learning of Esau's threats to kill Jacob, cooked up another plan. Esau's wives drove both Isaac and Rebekah nuts. That would be Rebekah's card to play. She convinced Isaac of Jacob's need to marry, but not one of those Canaanite women. He would go to Harran, to Rebekah's childhood home, and find a wife from Laban's family.

Jacob didn't have much warning before he fled. Neither did we in my own family situation. This is a week of lasts. The last week where we watch the fog roll up to the edge of land and turn the world white except for our bright green grass and trees. Today the fog cocoons us in the soft gauze of kind, cool mist.

The last week of waking to a wide-angle view of the world from atop our perch on the bluff. The last week of a birdsong from the custom birdhouse outside the windows. The last week in the kitchen I finally learned to love, the home I finally learned to create. The last week to sit in the yard and watch the sun's rising, light flitting on the water's ripples like sparklers on the Fourth of July, or the evening sunset striking the houses across the lake with fire and glow, a band of brilliant homes. Like heaven, I imagine, or a vacation.

The last week in this home after sixteen years of dawns spilling into our bedroom windows. Memories of raising three children haunt this place—our kids and their friends streaming across the yard playing Capture the Flag and Ghost in the Graveyard, roasting marshmallows and hot dogs around a bonfire as the sparks climb like tiny flashing stars. The shouts of laughter, the sweat, the rope-swing hung from the strong arm of the oak. Stubbed toes, a broken nose, kids in the tops of hundred-foot pines.

The last week in a home packed with the memories of our family, and the families who lived here before us, stretching back in time to the stagecoach route and all the stragglers who bedded down here for the night or for a week's getaway. The lines on the floor in the attic whisper stories, too, of times when seven guest rooms overlooked the water and offered an eagle's view of the morning and of rowboats on the lake called Gray. The oak trees were young, then, back in the 1880s. Now they reach a mile toward God and stretch heavy, thick limbs to heaven. Their leafy fingers flap praise to the Most High God.

Memories echo—of laughter, of joy, of singing "Up from the Grave" at the dining room table on Easter, or "Happy Birthday" on each person's special day, and always, always the circling of hands around that table for blessing and prayer. That table headed Tuesday to the thrift store, and for that alone I grieve. We raised our children around that table, spilled milk and filled-tummy groans after plentiful meals.

We made too many mistakes around that table, trying to learn how to parent and how to love in difficult places.

The last week to savor memories where they occurred, of us running barefoot down to the garden for warm tomatoes on the vine and tender lettuce. Or the forgotten lettuce, now like green stalks with tough parchment leaves. I can feel the soft grass, cool even on hot days but bristly in our summers of drought. The last week to remember the broomball and hockey games when the lake froze, the skiing when snow blanketed the hockey rink, the red noses and freezing toes. The shouts, the numb fingers, and the hot chocolate by the gallons.

And I grieve good grief for all the marvel here. And sad grief, the grief of mistakes lived out, the "if only" and "we should have" and "why didn't we?" that steal into my throat and choke me.

Not everyone gets a week's notice, and so, this week, what remains of it, I resolve to notice. The crowding memories, the beauty, the tears, the pealing joy. James 4:14–15 reminds us that, "You do not even know what will happen tomorrow. . . . You ought to say, 'If it is the Lord's will, we will live and do this or that.'"

So our resolve, yours, mine? To live, really live. This week? How about today?

TRAVELING MERCY

Dear one,
Not everyone gets a week
Or even tomorrow,
And there is plenty to savor
Every single day
Of your life.
So watch
And listen
And laugh
And forgive
And move forward.
And know that I am
Always with you
And with those you love
In spite of mistakes,
Of moments mis-lived,
Of regrets.
Let my love
Line the walls of your soul
And your memory bank.
Seal this time
With my assurance that
I am
God.

NOTE TO SELF

Love, listen, laugh, forgive. I can.

BLESSING ANYWAY

So Isaac called in Jacob and blessed him.

—GENESIS 28:1 MSG

After all the volleys of emotional fire between the Isaac family foursome, deep rifts might separate them all and lead to poor and petty choices. But Isaac, who'd missed the boat and blessed (he thought) the wrong boy, didn't let bitterness obscure better judgment.

When Rebekah wrung her hands over the sorry options for wives for her second-born son, knowing it was a good excuse to get Jacob to safety, Isaac set aside any personal ill-will between them and saw the sense in her words. She might not have understood the impact of her actions on the fledgling nation, but we can see, now, that had Jacob hung around and married a local girl or two, the family line might have disappeared into the tribes of the native people. Leaving Canaan set Jacob and all his hoped-for progeny apart from the Canaanites and their idolatrous ways.

Isaac refused to let his feelings stand in the way of the right next move. He could have been hurt, bitter, and ashamed. He could have felt rejected by Rebekah, or certainly double-crossed.

He could have wasted the next years of his life angry that the loving wife of his younger years had morphed into a seemingly scheming woman intent on her own way. He could have refused Jacob any relationship, held him at arm's length, and made no decisions about his future.

But Isaac, through with games, opened his eyes wide on reality. Though his physical sight had deteriorated, he saw the wisdom of sending away Jacob the deceiver. For everyone's sake, yes, but also for the sake of carrying forward the promise God made so many years ago to Abraham. In spite of all the dishonesty, Isaac wanted the best for his son. Isaac did more than send his heel of a son on his way. He blessed him, yet again.

Rather than running off, feeling their bitterness like a bottle broken over his head, Jacob left with these potent words of benediction pouring over him. Isaac, in spite of the past, sent his son away with this powerful reminder of his calling, his heritage, and the hopes for the future. Don't forget who you are, don't forget what God is doing, and don't get sidetracked in pettiness, but rather, pass on the blessing, keep rolling it forward everywhere you go.

In spite of the mess, Isaac chose to bless. He freed his son to live into his calling, to live into God's promise and up to his own potential. To learn what it meant to bless anyway. A beautiful example of recovery of vision and momentum, of leaning into the role of spiritual leader. I hope I can remember. I want to be like Isaac. Relinquish bitterness. Bless in spite of the mess.

TRAVELING MERCY
Dear one,
Don't forget who you are:
You are my child.
Don't get sidetracked
By blame and bitterness,
But rather,
Bless your way forward.

NOTE TO SELF
Bitterness sidetracks, blessing redirects.

ON YOUR MARK

So Isaac called in Jacob and blessed him. Then he
ordered him . . . "Leave at once."

—GENESIS 28:1 MSG

Jacob's escape forced him to learn to live in mid-flight, to
process and redirect as necessary even though on the run. As
the distance grew between himself and his angry brother, his
grieving mother, and his broken father, did he at last slow
down enough to breathe deeply? Once he stopped gasping for
air on the sprint out of Beersheba, maybe the panic cleared
his mind. In the wilderness, he could begin to address some
issues, though a painful process.

As much as we might dislike the wilderness, it creates
room, a chance to check the rearview mirror of our lives so we
can better envision and decide upon the route ahead. Surely
the distance from his former life offered an openness to honesty.
How long, for instance, did disappointment wait before its
pounce on Jacob? It must head up the list: disappointment with
others for the way they handled him and disappointment with
himself for his toxic damage to relationships.

Jacob could, of course, blame others for his actions, and
maybe he did. Rebekah, for her machinations. Isaac, for his

blind side that refused to see God's plan, revealed since the babies' gestation, or to notice the subterfuge all around him. Esau, for his lust that snagged both brothers like sheep's wool in barbed wire.

But Jacob was a grown man, no longer a teenager to lash out with a testosterone surge or a rash of impetuosity. Blame impedes growth. His best option included slicing through the cloak-and-dagger approach to receiving the inheritance and wielding that ancient tool of communication.

Looking back helps only if it enables us to turn our gaze inward, upward, and then forward. Otherwise, we trip over everything en route and get a kink in our neck—or break our neck. Dwelling on any disappointment with others should last only as long as it takes to say, "Oh, right, *imperfect* is the word for people this side of heaven. I keep forgetting. That hurts, or angers me, or . . . but I will heal." What else do we expect from anyone? Expecting perfection is like waiting for the sun to rise from the western horizon or dew to fall up instead of down. Expect and accept imperfection and the disappointment no longer impedes us, but rather lets us relinquish the hard feelings and bitterness that chase like bloodhounds on a scent.

Addressing that disappointment and then releasing others' roles in our lives frees us to focus on something we actually have power over: our own mistakes, our own poor choices, and our own options when we next shift the vehicle from reverse to drive. Honesty helps. In the middle of the desert, Jacob would be freed up of anyone else's actions or thoughts and be free to do the soul-research as to how he landed there on a flight-path to Harran.

As we journey through the wilderness, we can begin to accept imperfection and disappointment in others and in ourselves. And discover, en route, the freedom of relinquishment, which looks a lot like . . . forgiveness.

TRAVELING MERCY

Dear one,
Look back
But only so you can look within.
Look up
And then look forward
And around
At how to love others better,
How to forgive more quickly,
How to build
Rather than blame and break
Relationships.
Take time to consider
Your own role
And accept imperfection—
Yours
And others'.

NOTE TO SELF

Expect and accept imperfection.
Forgive fast and move forward.

UNNECESSARY KEEPSAKES

"Go at once."

—Genesis 28:2

Backpackers know the dangers of hauling too many supplies or too much weight in their packs. Even a lightweight satchel cuts ruts into your shoulders after a long day of travel. The heavier the backpack, the deeper the cuts, and the more the wilderness will cost you.

Wise travelers know what to leave behind, what they won't need en route. I'm not so wise, and the path from our current home is strewn with items too big to squeeze into our next house. Too much gear to carry with us. The ruts cut deeply into my soul, all this senseless weight to haul about. God is probably in heaven, Jesus shaking his head, the Holy Spirit sighing out an "I wish she'd listen sooner."

In the middle of a move, whether it's Jacob running to Harran or a job change or a transition in relationships, we so often carry too much to move well or fast. Or to move for long. And the wilderness is a long-distance commitment. To stop mid-desert is to invite death to drop in for a permanent layover.

What can we let go of on this leg of our journey? What weighs us down and cut ruts in our shoulders? Maybe our expectations of others who disappointed us? Or unforgiveness, sure to trip us when we run.

As I process this, I think I see, below the surface, a certain fear: We need our stuff because we can't replace it. We need it, why? Because God won't provide more? We need it, because no one else will ever give away or sell at the thrift store something we could use as replacement? Fear is so rarely rational, and this pierces and shames me. I should know better. For even as giveaways line the fence of our yard, so God's goodness fences our lives. All those giveaways were once gifts to us from God. We've never been in real need; we have always had food to eat, even if from four-for-a-dollar cans.

Everything we have came from God. And if God has called us—and surely that is the case, otherwise you and I should quit right now—then God will provide for us.

Isaac knew that, from the moment God provided a sacrifice on the altar. Jacob will learn that, as he runs from Esau toward a future with a new family and the building of a nation. Today, I will know it as I choose to prop my fear by the fence.

Hopefully, no one will want it.

TRAVELING MERCY

Dear one,
Leave it here
On the fence line—
Your fear,
Your unforgiveness,
Your failures.
You can't run the race
With that weight.
So leave them all here,
And let me fence you in
With my loving care,
My provision
My laughter,
My surprises.
We will travel together
And you can travel light.
I will pack the supplies.

NOTE TO SELF

What can I leave by the fence today?

A POWER LAUNCH

*May God Almighty bless you and make you fruitful
and increase your numbers.*

—GENESIS 28:3

Whatever Isaac's emotional cocktail after the various family intrigues were—guilt, shame, sorrow, anger, unforgiveness—he recognized the wisdom in sending away Jacob. To preserve the family line, set them apart from the local inhabitants, and save Jacob's life, Jacob needed to leave.

Isaac's emotional baggage didn't prevent him from giving a vital parting gift, a weightless gift to accompany Jacob on every adventurous step of his life. Weightless, at least, in its physical density, but worth a desert full of bullion. Isaac blessed his son. His scheming, deceiving heir. He prayed a downpour of blessing. That God would bless Jacob, make him fruitful, increase his numbers, and give those many descendants the blessings of Abraham. And he prayed that God would bring Jacob back to the land of promise, the land promised by the God who never breaks promises.

In spite of the masquerade, in spite of the rash of guilt. Isaac rose to his authority, conferring a spiritual heritage on another and refusing to bind his family with unforgiveness, blessed. This man trusted God even with a knife at his throat, learned to love in spite of abandonment, and chose to love again when abandonment and fear raised their heads.

Though Scripture mentions little blessing of Isaac by Abraham, in Isaac's blessing of his son, we see Isaac's spiritual depth and the results of God's blessings over him (Gen. 22:15–18). We witness this man's heart, who without physical sight saw clearly the spiritual necessity of blessing this now-heir. The God who saved him would in turn save his family line. Isaac had no idea what God would do in the future about his son's character, no idea the trials necessary to forge a new identity. Jacob would need that blessing.

Blessing requires freedom. To bless others, we must be freed from bitterness, unforgiveness, and anger. We cease holding others' weaknesses, mistakes, and sins against them, even though those bring (or brought) pain. To refuse to forgive leaves others vulnerable, susceptible to the arthritis of shame and further sin. Tightfisted, clenched by our own pain and its lack of resolution, we withhold the blessing of relationship, the gift of integrity, the wholeness that results from addressing and dressing wounds, then forgiving. We suppress the powerful calling down of God's abundance on another.

Imagine Jacob, who surely felt guilt over stealing the blessing of the firstborn. Lifting his hand over Jacob's head, Isaac said, in effect, "I forgive you. May God drop blessing from the storehouses and grow you."

Look at Isaac's deep trust of the God who calls, names, blesses, and saves. Isaac experienced all these aspects of God's character and now relayed them to Jacob.

Imagine that now for your soul. Perhaps no one ever blessed you. Hear Isaac's blessing over you, child of Abraham, child of God. Hear the words calling for fruitfulness, for increase, for a permanent home in God's heart. Let them soak into the parched soil of your insecurities, losses, and lacks.

God's blessing sets us free to bless. Jacob would learn this. And so will we. May we live into and out of the blessing of being loved, forgiven, and called by God.

TRAVELING MERCY

Dear one,
Perhaps no one blessed you.
Hear my words over you:
I love you.
A love with no beginning and no ending.
You mean the whole world to me.
You are my heir.
You are my joy.
You are my delight.
Live in that love
Rather than others' woundings.
Rather than the lack of blessings
From significant others.
Be freed by my love.
Then you're free
To free others
With forgiveness.
With hope.
With blessing.

NOTE TO SELF

Free to launch.

AUGUST DEVOTIONS

TO LEAVE WELL

Jacob left Beersheba and set out for Harran.

—GENESIS 28:10

Leaving well requires time. If Jacob really left with Esau frothing death threats at the back of his neck, panic determined his journey's speed. Panic, of course, leaves zero room for retrospect and a great deal of room for regret. Jacob was already primed for regret, given the mess of mixed motives and self-centered agendas of the family. But even for him, it was not too late to leave well.

Not too late for good to come from the snarled skein of relationships left behind. To leave well means that today we try to make yesterday's baggage a little bit lighter. That requires processing time, rather than a panicked pace. One thing the wilderness offers? It's long on time. Time to look back, to rethink (or in Jacob's case, to think for perhaps the first time). Our past needn't determine our future: our course of actions, our attitude in relationships, or our attention to work.

In fact, the wilderness foray is the perfect occasion to reflect on what worked, what didn't work, and what to do differently the next time. Even if we left in a hurry, every single leaving offers us this same possibility. A time to deliberate—to think, ponder, consider, and weigh—and then to act deliberately rather than impetuously. Rather than to allow rash impulse or base greed to control us. A place, at last, of movement toward integrity, of wholeness.

But the deliberation is not just for when we land, when we're settled. That is the future. To leave well must also include how to live well, right now, in this in-between, not-quite-there spot. Living well en route to tomorrow. Otherwise we put off the decisions to be made right now about how to live well in this moment. That seems to be part of Jacob's trouble: If he'd made some decisions before the heat of the moment—the rich opportunity to gain a birthright for the cost of a bowl of stew, for instance, or the chance to snag the blessing before Big Bro gets back from the field—he'd never have been exiled. He could have left with his family waving him off with hankies and dabbing at tears, and a clear conscience to go find the wife of his dreams (or, to be more exact, the four women who would build up the nation yet to be named Israel).

But today is a new day. So we decide, now, how our past can inform our today. And then we can begin to frame how that same yesterday informs our tomorrow.

To leave well can start at any time, even years after the fact. Daily, we can begin anew: What worked? What didn't work? Where was my greed operating, or when was fear in charge? (Jacob surely had plenty of both.) Even if we left poorly, dashing into the wilderness in fear for our lives, now we claim today as a new day. A day to start again.

TRAVELING MERCY
Dear one,
Deliberate
And then act deliberately.
Think, ponder, and decide
How you will be
Yourself,
How you will live into
The day and the life before you.
Stop running and start thinking.
Today's a new start,
A head start,
On the rest of your life.

NOTE TO SELF
Today isn't yesterday.
Today, move toward integrity.

JACOB'S UNFOLDING

Jacob left Beersheba.

—GENESIS 28:10

After the relief of escaping his brother's rage, didn't Jacob wonder if he'd sawed off the limb too close to the tree and left himself freefalling into the unknown?

For some, unknowns represent excitement and adventure. Freedom! No shackles from family ties, whether those bindings came in the guise of morality, ethics, or a sense of personal duty. Irresponsible Jacob could flee his past and all the obligations of being part of the family of Abraham.

Others, when they leave the daily knowns, see the unknown next page of their lives as a do-over, a chance to write a new life, to compose a new chapter. But not everyone loves to write, to add pages to their life book. So perhaps both relief and uncertainty tremble within them—"Whew, a new chance" and also, "What if I botch this opportunity?"

Sometimes, however much we anticipate the next chapter, leaving is a painful tearing away from the life we've known and loved. But the wilderness flight forces us to see with new eyes, to evaluate our lives with clarity.

The messiness of Jacob's relationships resembled a wad of knotted string art. Choosing between fight and flight was a cinch. Easy to flee, but hard to land and duke it out with his soul.

Physically speaking, no doubt he traveled light. Scripture never references an entourage accompanying him, although perhaps such is assumed for people of means and stature. But emotionally, fear and guilt nipped at his heels and chased him. Fear of Esau, of course. And hopefully a certain amount of productive guilt. Unless his conscience had been scrubbed free of all morals and ethics, filed off like the serial numbers on stolen property. Romans 1 tells us that God's law is written on our hearts and bears witness to us of right and wrong, so presumably Jacob wasn't standing behind the door when God formed the seat of his soul.

After all, Grandfather Abraham lived until Jacob and Esau were fifteen. I bet Abraham saw these ornery twin grandsons, the rambunctious start of the nation God promised.

Surely Abraham delivered on God's charge: "I will bless you, and you will be a blessing." How lovely if, after sending off his third wife Keturah[1] and his concubines and all their children with gifts (see Gen. 25:6), Abraham chose to be part of Isaac's young family. Meet the new wife, pray for off-spring, bounce the answered-prayer babies on his knee, and tell them excerpts from the Amazing Adventures of Abraham.

Surely Abraham at least dug a moral foundation and layered the concrete blocks of wisdom, the mortar of God's calling for these boys, and Isaac built upon it. They didn't proceed to building a life, not right away, not until much journeying taught them more about faith, about living wholely and living holy.

But this is the way of growing up. Though Esau and Jacob were not youngsters when they deceived and threatened each other, like all of us they needed time for the lessons learned to meld with the school of life. And Jacob needed the perspective he could get only by leaving the tents of his birth and the complicated relationships there. Leaving forced him to begin to reckon with who he had been, who he'd become, and the person God might be creating him to be.

Jacob's story isn't over, and neither is our story, nor that of people we love more dearly than anyone in the world. The Scriptures hold out hope that if we start people off on the right path, when they are old, they will not depart from it (see Prov. 22:6). Getting to old, thankfully, takes a lifetime. However long that is, we have hope. Today, we can move toward whole and make our way to the end of the story.

TRAVELING MERCY
Dear one,
Your story continues
Until I lead you
Home.
So grow now,
Grow into who you really are.
Become who I see you to be.
Let yesterday help shape your tomorrow
By deliberate action
Today.

NOTE TO SELF
Moving toward whole.

NOTE

1. Evidently, Hagar was Abraham's legal wife, and Keturah his third wife. Jewish Midrash, the body of story and interpretation grown up to understand and explain the Hebrew Scriptures, considers Keturah to be Hagar with a new name, but we have no proof of that. Here, assuming they are two different women, we end up with three wives for Abraham.

DESERT RUSHING

"Be still, and know that I am God."

—Psalm 46:10

The airplane landed on the runway. People's cell phones rang, chimed, and sang as information streamed across the plane's portals to passengers who'd endured electronic disconnect for far too long. As soon as the door to the jet bridge opened, people leaped up and crowded into the aisles, worried that they'd . . . what? Be stuck on the flight forever?

For the past twenty minutes, or maybe for the entire four-hour trip, I'd fretted, anxious about my connecting flight. We landed two hours late, and I had no idea where or when or even if my flight might be. I identified with all the aisle crowders, and perched, tense, on the edge of my seat, waiting for a chance to lurch into the walkway with my heavy briefcase.

The flight attendants asked people who weren't in a hurry to hold back, to allow passengers with tight connections to exit the plane first. One man, whose bald circle shone above his muff of hair, seemed to be jiggling in his anxiety. "Are you in a hurry?" I asked.

He shrugged, clutching his carry-on, his jacket wadded over his arm. "I'm in a hurry even when I'm not in a hurry."

I looked at him again, struck by this profound statement. For this is true of me as well, and living in the wilds has only highlighted this tendency. I, too, am in a hurry even when I'm not in a hurry. This shows up in traffic even with huge margins of time for delays en route, even with no deadline for arrival and nothing urgent to accomplish and no one waiting on me. I'm in a hurry. Period.

While some flight connections hinge entirely on ten seconds, most events in our lives are not so time sensitive that we need to jeopardize our cardiovascular system by living at such a frantic pace, always in a hurry. Nor do we need to run over other people with the wheels of our agenda simply because we're afraid we'll miss the next moment of opportunity.

The journey to freedom is not a race. Hurrying can kill us. To travel in the wilderness requires wise pacing, restful stops along the way, a food wagon, and perhaps an entire support van of medical care and a cot.

Plus, it's hard to hurry in the desert. Our shoes fill with dirt, we get dehydrated, we stumble and chew sand, and we leave others engulfed in the sandstorm of our hurry.

I doubt haste will shorten the trip. If anything, it will cripple us, render us unable to see, let alone reach, where we're meant to be going all along. It hurts us emotionally, because we don't listen to our deep-seated fears and worries when we're concerned only with a race. And it hurts us spiritually, because it's hard to hurry and trust simultaneously.

Maybe the desert wants to reverse our rushing tendencies. We may, after all, be here a very long time. Maybe, just for a moment today, we can recognize our hurry-worry pace and halt the hustle. Just be still. We are not, after all, gods of our own wilderness. As we stop, we run into the truth of God's words. When we are still, we release our own agendas and desires to rule the wilderness. And recognize, again, that God is God.

And that, my friend, is a relief. And a resting place.

TRAVELING MERCY

Dear one,
All that running will sap your strength
And drain you of vitality.
Why do you run, run, run
In the desert?
And what would happen
If you really believed me when I tell you
"Be still"?
Here's what would happen:
You would know relief,
Rest, repose, freedom from striving,
Because
I am God.
Even here.
Especially here, in this desert,
In this lonely, deserted, frightening place.
I am God.
Please, be still
And know.

NOTE TO SELF

Walk, don't run. There is enough time.

HEAD-ON-A-STONE MOMENTS

When he reached a certain place.

—Genesis 28:11

After a few days on the run, Jacob's exhaustion caught up with him. Short on soft, he lay his head on a rock and fell into a deep sleep. And just in time, too, before regret and shame gnashed their teeth and gobbled up any hope he might have had. So when God came to him in the dream, God's first words to Jacob the Deceiver, the Heel, the Cheat, the Liar were not words of shame or of finger-pointing. No "How dare you, you louse of a son and brother?" Rather, God said, "I am the Lord, the God of your father Abraham and the God of Isaac" (Gen. 28:13). Not, "I've cut you off from your family and this is the end of the line for you, buddy." None of the recrimination we might expect for a guy who'd just lied and cheated his way into the family's pocketbooks and right out of the family tents. "I am," God said. I am here, I am in your presence, and I have come to you in the darkest night of your soul. I am here with you in your regrets, shame, and fear.

Then God reminded him of his history—that Jacob was not alone, freefalling through life. Nor was he, by his actions, excommunicated from his forebearers. He was part of a mighty lineage of people who trusted God and trekked after God. The God who called, the God who rescued, the God who provided, the God who blessed. All that, God said, "I am."

Consider the balm to the fleeing Jacob's soul, the rest this offered. How he must have relaxed under that night sky, as the stars blinked overhead, to know that his sin wasn't unforgiveable, his shame not irreversible. His family line was not lost to him. He hadn't managed to annihilate his blessing and calling after all, because why?

Because God. Because God, I Am, said so.

Wherever we stop, wherever our shame started, wherever and however we acted out our lying, cheating, hurting, dehumanizing selves—and none of us is exempted from that, no matter how much we know the Sunday school answers about Jesus—whatever has driven us to this place between a rock and heaven, God enters. God has never been afraid to enter human history and misery with heavenly mystery.

And that is our story, as well. Our God, our I Am, the same God of Jacob, of his father Isaac, of Abraham, comes to us in our shame, in our fleeing, in our conniving and our cheating. In our wreckage of relationships and our disastrous choices. No matter what came before, no matter what we've left behind. This day, this night, this head-on-a-stone moment is not to be wasted. We are meant to be right here, right now, otherwise we could not hear through our fears or see through our tears. We could not listen past our steep barrier of regret. No matter. All is not lost, our futures not destroyed. Our hope remains firm. Because?

Because God. Because God, I Am, said so.

TRAVELING MERCY

Dear one,
Head-on-a-stone moments,
Don't trade them for a moment
Because it is here
Right now
That you encounter what you've sought
All along:
My blessing,
My love,
My provisions for you.
Right here,
Right now,
I am your light in this dark place.
I am your way.
I am
Yours.
And you are
Mine.

NOTE TO SELF

God, help me see in the dark. Please.

AUGUST 5

NIGHT VISIONS

He stopped for the night because the sun had set.

—GENESIS 28:11

Sleeping in the countryside with stars a blanket overhead sounds a bit romantic. But predators prowl at night, and in Jacob's day, animals with sharp teeth and vicious appetites surely howled under that picturesque starlight. Long scaly things slithered in the dirt. Jacob resting his head on a stone, with little protection beyond a fire to warm him and to frighten those snapping jaws away, is a brilliant picture of just how comfortable this journey was shaping up to be.

For any of us in Jacob's shoes, the external predators might be just the beginning of the clamping teeth and snarling drools that terrorize our nights.

Wise man, stopping at night. Night travel alerts our enemies of our sleep-deprived presence and our exhaustion-slowed steps. But how frightening to stop, to trust enough to realize that without stopping, we fall prey to exhaustion, foggy thinking, and poor decisions.

But put your head on a pillow, whether of feathers or stone, and sleep disappears in a nightmare of memories and regret.

Or of fear, which amplifies every noise. These very real predators stalk us in the dark, thieves who would break in, steal, kill, and destroy. Yes, a wise man, to stop at night. But scary, to stop at night. One becomes vulnerable then to both outer and inner terrors.

These inner predators may be one reason we stay so busy, keep hiking—working—long after sunset, long after the melatonin levels should rise in our systems and turn on our sleepytime clock. We keep working and wasting away, doing and doubting, because if we don't work, who will? If we don't, how will we ever finish our list? We keep on because otherwise, tomorrow's list will be twice as long. So on we trudge as the dark overtakes us, beating us down in body and soul.

More than just our undones complicate our sleep-deprived status and our motives. To lie down removes some of our barriers, and sleeping removes even more. And then the nightmares, the toothy jaws, and the dark regrets steal from our souls and into our dreams.

In sleep, God begins to unscramble our complicated souls and thoughts. To create new cells in our bodies, yes, but also new space in our souls for growth. In sleep, we get to trust that God will blanket us with protection and gentle loving care, tending to the fires we've left burning from our waking hours.

When Jacob laid his heavy head on that stone pillow, he also put down the shield of self-protection and laid aside all his defenses. Like him, with our defenses lowered, we begin to be receptive again, at last, to God.

Into that act of trust, God appeared. For the first time in our records of Jacob, God spoke into his soul. Tonight, see what happens when you put your head on your pillow (the rock is optional). Maybe it's time for God to sing you to sleep.

TRAVELING MERCY

Dear one,
A stone for a pillow
Is better than a heart of stone.
And you will turn to stone,
Hardened by regret,
By overwork,
By loneliness,
By exhaustion.
So lay down your weary head,
Make your bed
Under the starry skies
Of my care.
And if you listen carefully,
You will hear me
Singing you a lullaby.

NOTE TO SELF

God sings to me in my sleep.
I hope I hear tonight.

PORTAL TO HEAVEN

[Jacob] had a dream in which he saw a stairway resting
on the earth, with its top reaching to heaven.

—GENESIS 28:12

In the movie *Thor*, the superhero drops from the heavens
via a portal, a passageway between heaven and earth. The
only way he could get to earth and reclaim his good name,
stolen by his own greed and also by his greedy stepbrother,
was to descend through the portal, find the hammer, and
prove his honor by pulling it from its roots in earth. With his
honor proven, he could return through the same portal.

Ancient mythology cites this sort of portal, this mysterious
entryway to heaven, sometimes picturing it as a ladder or a
staircase. Since forever, we've been looking for the same
portal to take us out of our human misery and into God's
presence. As human beings, created in God's image, the often
unrecognized longing never leaves us, this longing for
heaven, for God, for hope, whether we identify that longing
in those terms or not.

But our striving, our achieving, our one-upping, all our
superhero attempts at living—aren't these all attempts to
create that portal ourselves? Or at least to find the key to the

passageway so we can finally reach our own highest version of ourselves? Or maybe not even a goal. Rather, perhaps we strive for what we've been missing all along: the connection with God, that deep lonely cry of our soul that says, "Love me, please." I'm quite sure that many of our social ills are related to that bleating soul cry: a portal, a passage, a way out, a way up, please.

If we can serve enough, love enough, earn enough, work hard enough, or give enough, then maybe we will be enough in someone's sight, maybe even in God's. We seek to build our own staircase by our accomplishments, by what the apostle Paul would one day call "works." "For it is by grace you have been saved, through faith—and this is not from yourselves, it is the gift of God—not by works, so that no one can boast" (Eph. 2:8–9). As a good Jewish man, a man schooled by the best rabbis and tutors in the world, Paul knew all the rules. He knew that every one of those laws was intended to reinforce people's tenuous connection to God and to what they all hoped would mean salvation. Salvation by perfection. Salvation by keeping the law. Perfection, then, would become the portal.

But that proved to be impossible, year after frustrating, broken year, as all the generations after Jacob tried and failed and tried again. They ended up as slaves to others, slaves to sin, slaves to riches.

And the running and exile continued, all the way up to one day, between then and now, when an angel announced to a teenager, "You will have a child." And then to her beloved, "You will be a father." And nine months later, to a field of shepherds. The portal between heaven and earth, closed since Jacob's time and even then inaccessible for us groundlings, opened through the birth of an infant.

Never would the portal work from earth to heaven—not by us, by our achievements on God's behalf or to impress God. Only by the Christ, who would return from heaven again, promising us his forever presence and through him forever access into the Holy of Holies, a "new and living way opened for us through the curtain" (Heb. 10:20).

The portal Jacob saw would, many years and generations later, be opened by the Lord Jesus, the long-awaited Messiah, the Son of David, the son of Judah—Jacob's great-great-great-great-grandson.

For all of us. A new and living way. Put away the reward charts and the earnings statements. We don't need them. The portal is open, and by God's amazing kindness, we can enter. Not on our net worth, but on Christ's.

Jacob must be beside himself with joy. Who could imagine a better outcome, with his background?

The door is open. Come on in.

TRAVELING MERCY

Dear one,
You can't imagine,
You will never know
How delighted I am
To welcome you into my presence,
And what it cost us
To open the portal from heaven to earth,
So you could enter heaven from earth
Not because you pulled the hammer from stone
By your worth,
But because of my Son—
The advent of his birth
And death
And life again.
The door is open.
Please
Come in.

NOTE TO SELF

Today I can cease striving on the inside.
God has opened the portal.

WHEN ANGELS APPEAR

[Jacob] had a dream in which he saw a stairway resting on the earth . . .
and the angels of God were ascending and descending on it.

—GENESIS 28:12

Never, never believe that because of our status or situation in life, God overlooks us. Hagar, from her low rung on the social ladder and abject hopelessness, is the first woman recorded in Scripture to interact with an angel. And not just once, but twice God pulled her from her misery in the wilderness through an angel's help and directive (see Gen. 16:7–12; 21:17).

Hagar is the first woman to name God (Gen. 16) and the first woman since Eden and sin's grand entrance, to hear God's voice directly. God spoke to Sarah through Abraham, but spoke to Hagar from heaven. The angel was God's emissary, then and throughout the Bible.

Angels intervened in Lot's decaying and far-from-admirable life, helping evacuate his family from Sodom. Years later, Abraham told his servant when he sent him to Harran to find a wife for Isaac, "God will send his angel ahead of you" (Gen. 24:7 MSG).

When Jacob lay his weary head on the stone for a pillow, in a dream a stairway descended from heaven, with angels coming and going, carrying out missions under God's directives. Angels perform significant work throughout the Scriptures, directing life, saving life, speaking life, delivering life.

We aren't to worship angels, nor do we become angels (a not-uncommon idea among some faith seekers). Psalm 8:5 says, "You have made them a little lower than the angels and crowned them with glory and honor." We can stop waiting for our wings, but here's a wonder: Jesus tells us of our value with his words, "See that you do not despise one of these little ones. For I tell you that their angels in heaven always see the face of my Father in heaven" (Matt. 18:10).

If you have felt alone, you are not alone. If you've felt abandoned or despised, you are not alone. If you have been frantic for direction, you are not alone. Whether we are despised or delighted in by others, God sends angels, God speaks through angels, and God appoints angels over us all. In all our hopeless places, we have no idea how much unseen help we're receiving from heaven, whether by angels or the power of the Holy Spirit. Or both.

One woman, in the lowest point of her life, mothering tiny children and battling depression, propped herself up in a restaurant with her family. An elderly man hobbled to her, pointed a finger in her face, and said, "You are a very good mother. These children are well-behaved and well-loved." Then he walked back to his window table. My friend sat, astonished, the light of life beginning to prick holes in the dark wall of her depression. As she and her husband prepared to leave, the man disappeared. One moment he was framed by the window's brightness, then in their next glance, gone.

Back in the car, my friend's husband said, "It isn't every day that you get to meet an angel, is it?" And this mother, hanging on by a thread, grabbed the rope thrown her by that angel of a man, and held on.

So do we. We grab the rope; we cling tightly. Whether via an angel unaware or an angel who looks like someone you know, God sends help. May God open our eyes to see, and our ears to hear.

TRAVELING MERCY
Dear one,
Angels go before you.
I send them to do my bidding.
You are constantly
Under my care
And protection.
So hold tight.
Grab the rope.
Know this,
I'm with you for good
And forever.

NOTE TO SELF
I can hold on to God.
A moment at a time.

JUST IN TIME

"I will not leave you until I have done what I promised you."

—GENESIS 28:15

We think that we are alone in our misery, surrounded only by the bleak loneliness and terror of midnight in those unknown, desolate places. That no one knows what is happening in our lives. In the middle of the night or the dark of pre-morning, the aloneness and the pain overwhelm us, like floods in the basement of our souls, with rain leaking through all the barriers we've carefully erected.

And then we learn that someone was praying furiously for us during that travail. Never, ever believe the lie that says, "You are alone. No one knows. Therefore no one cares." It is a foul-breathed deception from our dragon-mouthed Enemy who tried to convince Adam and Eve so many centuries ago that God didn't have their best interests at heart.

Didn't Jacob feel alone on his wilderness run? Didn't he feel the misery, the regret? If he had any sort of heart, no way could he entirely evade or avoid sorrow. Or fear. In the desert, alone, he, like all of us, was prey to the entire panorama of emotions.

But that night in the wilderness, after Jacob left his past with its mistakes and his loved ones behind, God visited him in a dream. Just in time, God met him in the dark as the stars poked holes in the thick, black sky.

God will meet us, as well, in the dark places of our lives. Just in time. Will it look like a stairway to heaven? A mystical appearance? Angels ascending and descending? Yes, no, maybe. But God will meet us because the promise God made for Jacob holds throughout the ages.

No matter the thickness of the dark or the depth of our misery, we are not alone. Whether God appears in a dream or remains unseen, his words to Jacob apply to us, as well: "I will not leave you until I have done what I have promised you" (Gen. 28:15). God will not leave us. Try it again, using first person singular, because God's Word is personal and permanent: God will not leave *me*. To this promise we return day after a day, and night after night: God will not leave us. Jesus reiterates this promise in Matthew 28:20: "Surely I am with you always, to the very end of the age." And later, "Never will I leave you; never will I forsake you" (Heb. 13:5).

When will God leave us?

Never. We can sleep on that.

Whether on a stone or a pillow or our rucksack, we can rest our heads and sleep on that promise. Hear it again: "I will not leave you until I have done what I promised you."

TRAVELING MERCY

Dear one,
Despite the floods and rains,
The misery and cold
The long nights
Sleeping on a stone pillow,
You are not alone.
I repeat:
You are not alone.
I have angels covering you,
People praying for you,
And I am with you
Always,
Even to the end of the age,
Which never ends.

NOTE TO SELF

Sleep in peace. God covers me.

FAMILY TREE

"I am the LORD, the God of your father
Abraham and the God of Isaac."

—GENESIS 28:13

Not everyone swings from a family tree like Jacob's, with branches thick and strong (and famous). Not everyone bears the third-generation DNA of Abraham and Isaac, with all the gifts inherent. So maybe God's blessing over Jacob means less to you than it could. When God says, "I am the God of Abraham and Isaac," you could shrug your shoulders and say, "Well, that's irrelevant to me, because I dangle by a twig from a truly messed-up family tree."

Maybe you wish you'd had such strong leaders in your family, people who'd raised you from the womb to worship the strong God, the God who provides, and the God who sees. If only that were the case, you think, your life's trajectory would be flying on a beautiful direct path toward heaven, a veritable zipline, and the landmines you've tromped through would never have detonated. Because you'd have been rooted and grounded in a faith that you'd never have run from.

At least, that's what we tell ourselves in the ambush moments that regret and disappointment send our way.

So you didn't have people who taught you about God and brought you to God. Abraham's family worshiped idols, as did everyone around him, and God still took hold of him. Or you had people who spouted the right words but lived the wrong life message toward you. That is surely a detriment to a strong start on life. Jacob's parents and grandparents tried to love and serve this God but still failed in significant ways, failed to straighten out the heel-grasper. But Jacob still ran, and ran smack into the living God.

So whether your roots are firmly planted in a generations-long list of faithful followers of God or not; whether you grew up learning Bible stories in Sunday school and reciting all the books of the Bible in order or not; whether you prayed around your family table or not—wherever you are is where God will find you.

Having a "better" or different past provides no guarantee of a bigger faith or a stronger foundation. Neither does having a difficult past guarantee a disastrous future. God is bigger than the good and the bad in your past.

In the game of hide-and-seek, God always finds us. We cannot escape. We can run, but thankfully we'll never hide from this God of the heavens, this God of Abraham, Isaac, and Jacob. So however you landed with your head on a rock in the middle of a field in the middle of the night, you're in the right place for God to speak, for God to appear, and for God to reassure.

Whatever is past, is past. Thank God for the past, because it helped form you in ways you cannot yet imagine. Where you are, right now, is the right place.

TRAVELING MERCY
Dear one,
You cannot be
Where you are not,
And you cannot be
Who you are not.
Your past does not stop me
From finding you,
Loving you,
Healing you,
Leading you.
Stone pillows
Are my way
Of finding you.

NOTE TO SELF
My past brought me to today.
I'm in the right place.

LONG-TERM PLAN

"I will give you and your descendants the land
on which you are lying."

—Genesis 28:13

The surprise and gift, totally undeserved and unexpected, of Isaac's blessing still rang in Jacob's ears. For wasn't he surprised, after all his deception, to have ended up with the sincere and knowing blessing of Isaac over him? This time Isaac knew exactly what he was doing, if there was any doubt before. This time Isaac didn't have to pretend he was blessing Esau rather than Jacob. This time, Isaac could genuinely and wholeheartedly give Jacob a blessing for the future (see Gen. 28:3–4).

By the time Jacob bedded down for the night, after his trek from Beersheba, perhaps he'd run the gauntlet of his mind and his past enough to stockpile some measure of peace, given his current status. Alone, separated from his parents, his brother, his past, and what he'd always assumed to be his future. To leave home after such deception, with a genuine blessing, would be enough for most of us, and probably for Jacob.

But then God's appearance into his dreams added another layer of faith and hope, another layer of promise and responsibility to Jacob's life. After establishing the lineage of faith in Abraham and Isaac, God said, "I will give you and your descendants the land on which you are lying." In other words, God was saying, "Jacob, you can run, but you will return here, you and your family, and the promise I made to your grandfather and to your father holds for you as well. You will return and bring your people, and you will be a nation. Your past failures are not fatal, nor will I rescind the promise I made many years ago to bless Abraham and all of his people down to you, and then through you."

There was Jacob, flat out in that field, neck stiff from resting his head on a rock, when smack into the middle of Jacob's dream, God revealed the long-term plan. In great kindness, God promised him a return to the very land he fled. What a relief. God reminded him, stabilized him, and staked a claim on him for the future. Just as God reminded Jacob of his history, so now God reminded him of his heritage.

How many are the nights when we bed down in the agony of regret and failure? And how many are the nights when God waits for us there, in our rock-hard place, ready to encourage us? When our deception catches up with us, when our thievery chokes us, when we turn away from our past and our loved ones in an attempt to save ourselves? How many are the nights when God hopes we will open our hearts to the healing truth of his presence and promise for us, and his reminder of the heritage in store for us and those we love, for all who love God?

Whether we leave a plugged nickel or a stash of stocks and bonds for those who come after us, our real heritage is this: We have been loved by the God of the universe, the God who called Abraham, who called Isaac, who called Jacob, and now calls us by name.

In these darks nights, God comes and reminds us, as well: "Don't forget. This is all for you. So get back here. You have some blessing to do."

TRAVELING MERCY

Dear one,
You are part of a long line
Of blessing,
And this stony place
Is a step along the way,
Only a section
Of my long-term plan.
You will return
A changed person,
And you will live into
Your new name
And the hopes I have
For you
And those who follow you.
Start today?

NOTE TO SELF

Loving others is the inheritance I give and leave after me.
A good trail.

PRESENCE AND PROMISE

"I am with you and will watch over you wherever you go,
and I will bring you back to this land. I will not leave
you until I have done what I have promised you."

—Genesis 28:15

For a man on the run, Jacob's final revelation from God in this pivotal dream gave him fresh legs for sprinting the rest of the journey. All the previous words God spoke about the growth of the nation—dust of the earth! But now, comes the great truth of God's unwavering presence and the faithfulness of his promise. This is more than the cherry on top; this is the entire entree and the flaming dessert in the wilderness.

Didn't the totality of God's promise wash over Jacob in wonder? The forgiveness: the nation will continue to grow, and spread, and blessing upon blessing will cascade across the earth, unhindered by Jacob's sinful acquisition of the birthright and blessing. On top of all that, God told this deceiver, the one who fled from his past toward an unknown and uncertain future: "I am with you and will watch over you wherever you go."

God, the I Am, with him. Watching over him, everywhere. How comforting to a man who worried if he'd be murdered in his sleep, if he'd ever find a wife or household or a future whatsoever.

And then, that Jacob, after all, would indeed be the spiritual head of his family—imagine, God honoring that stolen birthright!—as well as father an entire nation of people, descendants like the dust of the earth.

Jacob awoke, wide-eyed with awe, and said, "Surely the LORD is in this place, and I was not aware of it" (Gen. 28:16). Isn't that the truth for all of us? Isn't God's promise to us the same as to Jacob? "I am with you." Not, I *will be* with you or I *might be* with you. I *am* with you. I AM. We are not alone. Not ever on our own, but God is with us. We don't need to pray, "God, be with me today." God laughs at the redundancy—God is already with us. God isn't going to leave us without him, and we aren't going anywhere without God.

I shake my head at this, amazed and humbled. For I am Jacob, and you are Jacob, and still, God is with us and will watch over us wherever we go.

Jacob sat upright after this dream and proclaimed, "How awesome is this place! This is none other than the house of God; this is the gate of heaven" (28:17). He established his stone pillow as a pillar and poured oil on top, anointing it, and called the place Bethel, House of God. Hear the depth of Jacob's commitment in his next words: "If [or *since*, in Hebrew] God will be with me and will watch over me . . . will give me food . . . and clothes . . . so that I return safely to my father's household, then the LORD will be my God . . . and of all that you give me, I will give you a tenth" (Gen. 28:20–22).

Jacob began to walk out his spiritual heritage, following his grandfather Abraham's vow to give a tenth of his possessions.

In fact, the next phrase, "Then Jacob continued on his journey," literally means "and Jacob lifted up his feet." An unusual expression in the Hebrew that undoubtedly means that he moved forward with new energy and zest. Fresh legs, indeed. Legs of faith, legs to carry him into the future.

Oh, if only we, too, were so stricken by God's presence in this place, wherever we are! Here, right here, right now— that we, too, vow that the Lord will be our God. And return a tenth of all God gives us, right back to him.

Imagine that. Churches would never need another fundraiser, another pancake sale, or another booth at the fair. From overflowing coffers, God's work would infiltrate the world, blessing. And blessing. And blessing some more.

TRAVELING MERCY
Dear one,
Lift up your feet.
I give you fresh legs,
Energy to run the race.
I am in this place
And so are you.
So let's run forward together.
Walk out your spiritual heritage,
A tithe on your life
Flowing into the world.

NOTE TO SELF
God's presence gives fresh legs of faith.
Get ready to run.

HOME AWAY FROM HOME

"You are my own flesh and blood."

—GENESIS 29:14

On those fresh legs, Jacob powered through his travels, possibly another two hundred or more miles, and came to the "land of the eastern peoples." He trod the right path, and the first people he met there at the well in open country were shepherds, waiting for all the various flocks and herders to arrive to divvy up the precious water supply fairly.

Jacob asked, "My brothers, where are you from?"

Wouldn't you know, they were from Harran, the land of his mother's people? Jacob continued his questions: "Do you know Laban, Nahor's grandson?" That should narrow the available family trees, if there were many Labans lounging around Harran.

Of course they knew that particular Laban. Isn't God leading? So Jacob inquired, kindly, about Laban's health. The question reads, "Is he well?" in the NIV, but the original language literally means, "Is there peace to him?" (see Gen. 29:6).

Though the shepherds nodded, we will soon begin to wonder as we continue the story just how much peace there was for

Laban. He was, truly, Jacob's mother's brother, and the trickery we saw from Laban when Abraham's trusted servant
readied Rebekah and her maid for the journey to Isaac was a
sneak preview of his true character.

So far, so good: Jacob made it to the right city and the
right family. God was with him! He must have marveled at
this amazing direction.

But then, Laban's daughter, a shepherdess, walked into Jacob's
life. When Jacob saw her, he ran over to the well, rolled away
the stone singlehandedly, and in a fever of urgency and grace
watered his uncle's sheep. This gift accomplished, he kissed
Rachel and wept right out loud. Family. He had found his family. After leaving his mother behind, how comforting this
must have been for Jacob to meet his cousin, his mother's
(and his own) flesh and blood.

In fact, we see this through the emphasis in the Hebrew.
While the NIV says simply, "Laban" in Genesis 29:30, in the original language, he is twice introduced in verse 30 as "Laban, the
brother of his mother." We don't learn, yet, that Rachel was
beautiful. Only that Laban, the brother of Jacob's mother, owned
these sheep and Rachel was his daughter. And Jacob wept.

His tears, so uncharacteristic, clue us into the state of his soul.
God was at work in him.

Rachel, learning that Jacob was Rebekah's son, ran for her
father, who hurried out to meet Jacob. Laban, all unctuous
welcome, embraced and kissed him and brought him home.
Laban sized up Jacob, declaring, in the original Hebrew as
though he'd needed to be convinced (like, "Ah, OK, I believe
it now"): "Indeed, my bone and my flesh are you."

The answer to Jacob's statement made while he bedded down on the stone he named Bethel, "If God will be with me . . ." begins to be obvious. The Lord was with him on his journey. Good thing. He will need God's presence, because the first "month of days" will end all too quickly.

From Bethel "house of God" to the house of Laban, Jacob traveled, always seeking home. For now, we all rest contentedly (though not for long). Jacob found the very family he sought. His God, who appeared to him in a dream in a field in the midnight of his life, led him straight into the middle of their sheep and then to their arms and then to their home.

And we, like Jacob, chase home, learning, ultimately, that home is wherever God dwells.

TRAVELING MERCY
Dear one,
There's a welcome mat
For you
Right here,
Right now.
For where you are,
I am,
And you are always
Home.
Because I am
Always with you.
Right place.
Right family.

NOTE TO SELF
My home is where God is. Right here.

SEVEN-YEAR SWITCH

"I'll work for you seven years in return for
your younger daughter Rachel."

—GENESIS 29:18

Jacob evidently turned his shoulder to the plow (or his leadership to the herds) immediately on camping at Laban's home. But in spite of the workload, he had time to fall in love with Rachel, who, parenthetically, we learn is Laban's younger daughter and gorgeous. Depending on the version we read, Rachel's sister Leah was unlovely, had bad eyes, or had fine eyes. The Hebrew word means "delicate" or, as translated in the NET Bible, "tender" (Gen. 29:17), whatever we take that to mean.

Regardless, Leah was no competition for her sister, who was "lovely of form and appearance" (I guess they are not the same thing). Jacob had eyes only for Rachel. When Laban inquired about paying Jacob and making his servitude official—perhaps a son wouldn't be paid for the work—Jacob played his heart card.

"I will work for seven years for your daughter Rachel." Jacob, from a wealthy family but with no inheritance yet in his hands, was impoverished. He entered Harran with only a staff (Gen. 32:10). With no bride price, he instead offered his labor to Laban. At a shekel of silver per month for pay, Jacob's seven years of work represented eighty-four shekels—just about double the going bride price of thirty to forty shekels.

Pretty steep offering, and Laban was quick to jump. His eyes narrowed and he stroked his beard, the cash register *ca-chinging* in his head. The years "seemed like only a few days to Jacob because of his love for her" (Gen. 29:20) and flew by. Finally he insisted to Laban, "Give me my wife. My time is completed, and I want to make love to her" (v. 21). Nothing like getting the truth out in the open.

By then, he was at least forty-seven, his brother was way ahead with a passel of wives and children, and it was time to get that nation started.

Jacob, who seemed to be trying to fly right, was about to get his wings nipped. His boss and future father-in-law again turned shrewd and held a wedding feast. That first night, while Jacob waited in his tent for his beloved, Laban sent in Leah, the firstborn daughter. Only in the morning, after the marriage was consummated and pitch dark gave way to day did Jacob, the reforming deceiver, learn that he had been deceived, and royally. He found in his arms, not Rachel, but Leah.

What goes around, comes around, and Jacob who stole the rights of the firstborn son ends up with the firstborn daughter for a wife. It doesn't seem fair, but life rarely is, and besides, we need a nation and we need one fast. It all came together, but not without damage and loss of trust. Laban agreed to give Rachel at the end of the wedding week (very possibly long enough for Leah to conceive), so Jacob had not one but two wives. Oh, and another contract for seven more years of labor.

The sorry part of the story is that Leah, the one with tender eyes, had eyes for her husband, but he could not see her for Rachel's beauty. The sibling rivalry between Jacob and Esau repeats itself in the lives of Rachel and Leah.

God, who is tender toward those who are under-loved, blessed tender-eyed Leah with four boys in rapid succession.

God brings good out of the most amazing and unusual circumstances, factoring in Laban's greed, Jacob's deceit, and the bitter competition between the wives. God will build that nation out of the only building blocks available: fallen people.

And that's the good news for today. You, me, Jacob, Laban. Fallen people become the family of God.

TRAVELING MERCY
Dear one,
I have eyes for you,
Tender eyes,
And have spent your whole life
Moving you toward
Me.
You are part of the building crew,
Building the family of God
One fallen person
At a time.
I've never had such joy.
I'm so glad you're part of
The family.

NOTE TO SELF
I am a builder. Not perfect, but growing.

SERIOUS WORD PLAY

"This time I will praise the LORD."

—Genesis 29:35

Laban, whose wife seemed to have been MIA, named his girls after agrarian interests. *Leah* means "cow," "gazelle," or "wild cow." Maybe I'd go with gazelle or wild, and forget the cow. Rachel was named, rather more kindly, but also fitting for a shepherd, "ewe." Auntie Rebekah was named after a choice calf. Let's hand it to the family, naming all the girls after farm animals.

Isaac means "laughter," *Jacob* means "heel grasper," *Esau* means "hairy," and *Laban*, for whatever reason, means "white." When his grandchildren start squalling their way into the world, their names will be significant given the surrounding circumstances.

At her first son's birth, Leah with delicate eyes said, "Look, a son!" (the meaning of Reuben's name). "The Lord has looked with pity on my oppressed condition." The nuances in Hebrew are rich with drama and irony. But her next words wring my heart: "Surely my husband will love me now" (Gen. 29:32 NET).

Baby number two, Simeon, was named after Leah's words at his birth, too: "The Lord has heard that I was unloved." Simeon, from the root meaning "hearing." Boy 1 was "God sees"; boy 2 was "God hears." Baby boy 3 was Levi. "Now this time my husband will show me affection, because I have given birth to three sons for him." *Affection* literally means "will be joined"; so Jacob "will be joined" to Leah (well, the Hebrew is succinct, at least), and the root word for Levi sounds like the same verb, "to join." Baby 3, loves.

Leah hoped in vain for her husband's love, although Jacob probably wasn't having too dismal a time of it. A fourth child followed and Leah made a significant decision regarding names. She declared, "This time I will praise the Lord." *Judah* means, "He will be praised."

This son was the only son so far that she hasn't named in hopes of attention from her husband. In spite of her less-than-loved status, Leah determined that would praise God.

From the tribe of Judah, "God be praised," would be born David, the last-born son of his father, Jesse, but the spiritual head of the clan according to Scripture. And from David would be born Jesus the Christ, the firstborn son, David's "greater son."

Psalm 22:3 tells us God inhabits our praise, and we see this truly lived in, and out, via the naming of Leah's fourth son. Many generations later, with the Lion of Judah's birth, life, death, and resurrection, we, too, are included in the tribe of Judah. We become people who declare, "God be praised," whatever our circumstances, wherever we find ourselves.

This sounds good. But today, praise ranks dead last on my agenda. We creep among boxes, an unsorted kitchen, office contents spread around a city block, and offices entirely unready for habitation and work. We are sleep deprived and still, in spite of all this, need to stay faithful to God's work and calling. I stretch out on the rug in my office, the heat rendering me numb and fuzzy. And perhaps a little angry.

I do not want to say, "God be praised." I don't want to tune the strings on my heart to sing my prayers. I want to burrow, preferably in the cool dark with fresh coffee and chocolate, and not have to participate in today.

I am Jacob, Esau, Leah, Rachel, all of us in some sort of pain, all of us wanting our lives to change. And I decide, that for the moment, I will choose to be like Leah at Judah's birth. God be praised. I walk for ten minutes, outside, skirting the sun and sticking to the shade of the large leafy trees. And I praise everything I can think of about God. Every sound, every scent, the new keys in my pocket. I return, grateful, my heart again changed.

This time, like Leah, I will praise the Lord.

TRAVELING MERCY

Dear one,
I'm loving the sound
Of your praise,
Of your attention
To all the work I've put into
This world
For you.
Stick to the shade
Of those large leafy trees.
Find me beside you
In the cool shadows,
In the warm sun,
In the packed boxes,
And in the scent of
The lilies blooming
Along your walk.
Breathe deeply.
I love the sound
Of your joy.

NOTE TO SELF

Praise turns me from self to centered.

A DEEP BREATH

God sets the lonely in families.

—Psalm 68:6

In the midst of all this fertility that isn't her own, the loved Rachel turns green with jealousy and grips her husband's lapels: "Give me children or I'll die!" Jacob misses his chance to pray for his beautiful and beloved wife, and instead reacts. The original reads, "And the anger of Jacob was hot." "Am I in the place of God who has kept you from having children?" (Gen. 30:2 NET).

Desperate, barren Rachel resorted to the cultural practice of surrogacy and offered her servant Bilhah to Jacob as a third wife, which would only further complicate the family dynamics. "Sleep with her so that she can bear children for me": literally, the Hebrew phraseology is "upon my knees." Bilhah the servant would bear the children and place them upon her mistress's knees, signifying Rachel's adoption of the children and Bilhah's role as surrogate mother. But hear Rachel's plaintive cry, "so that I too can build a family." To be loved and beautiful is not always enough; Rachel wanted children, and like many women before and after her, adoption offered a deep fulfillment of that longing.

Fertile Bilhah bore a son; Rachel named him Dan, "judge," the root meaning "vindicated." His name highlights Rachel's sense that God was righting the wrong of her infertility. Before long, Bilhah, whose name might mean "untroubled," sure appears to have been untroubled by barrenness and again conceived. Tellingly, Rachel cited her own rivalry with and victory over her sister as the basis for that son's name: Naphtali, "struggle." His name reflects Rachel's "mighty struggle" (so big, the Hebrew literally reads, "struggles of God") to bear children.

Leah would bear more children. And Rachel, as much as she longed for her own children, remained barren for many years. At long last, "God remembered Rachel; he listened to her and enabled her to conceive" (Gen. 30:22). The son born to her and Jacob she named Joseph, not for his sake but rather as an expression of her deepest longing for yet another child. "May the Lord add to me another son," Rachel said. Joseph means, "May he add." One child from her own body was not enough.

The cultural pressure to give birth, to raise children, and to add to the family line was immense in those days and placed Rachel's femininity and worth at stake.

In some ways, this remains unchanged. To be childless in church today is to sit in a pew, embarrassed, on Mother's Day, or to skip worship that day. Too often, to be childless is to be judged, found wanting. People will say you're selfish, you're not a real woman, or you can't imagine what you're missing. Any shift from what the people of God consider the norm leaves us as pariahs, unaccepted and unacceptable.

For today, let's suspend judgment. There's more than enough pain to go around, and not nearly enough kindness and mercy.

Perhaps you are the one judged, because you have no children, whether by situation, choice, or infertility. Perhaps you are the one judging, because you know exactly what a perfect family looks like.

Today, let's stop and breathe. God has always been the one who sets the lonely in families. Families that God designs. Surely God designed the church as part of that family. Today, we learn to listen and feel with our hearts another's pain. And we love, a little bit more, today.

TRAVELING MERCY

Dear one,
I set the lonely—
You and your neighbor
And the woman in the pew
Next to you—
In families.
Can you suspend judgment
And become family
For one another?
To love, uphold, nourish, tend,
Just like I
Love, uphold, nourish, and tend
You?
And then the world will know
How family really looks.
They will want to be adopted
Into your family tree.

NOTE TO SELF

Breathe, love, repeat.

SO (UN)HAPPY TOGETHER

Be devoted to one another in love. Honor one
another above yourselves.

—ROMANS 12:10

In Jacob's family, we now have far more than the original triangle of Jacob, Rachel, and Leah. Add in two surrogate mothers (and wives numbers three and four), Bilhah and Zilpah, and then throw narrow-eyed Laban into the figure, and we have a hexagon. Navigating these dynamics would confuse anyone, but Rachel and Leah ruled the roost and seem to at least have had their servants under control if not their own sisterly relationship.

It's exhausting to keep track of the hexagon and then the children popping into the world. Leah realized, after Bilhah bore Naphtali for Rachel, that her own womb had stopped making babies, so she gave her servant Zilpah to Jacob as a wife . . . and a surrogate. (Four boys not being enough, evidently.) Zilpah gave birth to Gad, a "fortunate" birth, and then again to Asher, the happy one. "How happy am I," Leah exclaimed, "The women will call me happy" (Gen. 30:12–13 NET). Six boys for Leah, four by birth and two via surrogacy, two adoptions for Rachel. Four more boys to go.

And then Reuben, out picking flowers for his mother, Leah, brought in the popular mandrake plant, considered an aphrodisiac. Why he thought his mother needed this, who can say? He was old enough to realize her unloved status. When Rachel learned of those plants, though, she demanded them from Leah.

Leah charged. "Wasn't it enough that you stole my husband? Will you take my son's mandrakes too?" (Gen. 30:14–15).

Rachel and Leah swapped: Rachel got the mandrakes and Leah bought a night with her husband. Before he could take off his work boots, she met him, agenda-ready: "Sleep with me. I have hired you with my son's mandrakes" (v. 16).

Obliging as ever, Jacob slept with Leah, she conceived, and bore a fifth son. Leah viewed this child as a reward from God for giving Zilpah to Jacob, and named the boy Issachar, meaning "man of reward."

Ironically, Rachel traded Jacob for the mandrakes in order to conceive, and again, Leah became pregnant. "God has presented me with a precious gift. This time my husband will treat me with honor, because I have borne him six sons," Leah proclaimed. If only it worked that way. She named him Zebulun, "honor," in hopes of respect and love from her husband.

Beautiful and loved Rachel, unfulfilled as a mother, and Leah, a tent full of children and unfulfilled as a wife. They each had what the other sought, and rather than coming together in their grief, they lived in contention and competition with one another.

Isn't it so in our lives? Competition, like what came between Rachel and Leah, continues even today. We see it in the church, in the workplace, and in families. In our own broken-heartedness, we covet others' blessings, their gifts or talents, without recognizing the pain they carry. We fail to realize that together, we all make one complete whole. In all of our striving, we are Rachel, we are Leah, we are broken, and we need one another. Not to take what is not ours, but rather, to journey together. Stronger together. Happier together.

TRAVELING MERCY

Dear one,
Weep with those who weep,
Laugh with those who laugh,
Learn to love without competing,
Begin to serve without wanting,
And you will be becoming;
And joyful laughter will ring
From your rafters,
And you will learn
What life in heaven
Will be like.

NOTE TO SELF

Competition divides; love completes.
Choose love today.

IN ALL HONESTY

"My honesty will testify for me in the future."

—Genesis 30:33

At least fourteen years pass, full of contention and crying and a ton of testosterone in Jacob's tents. The tally thus far of sons born to Jacob's four wives:

- Leah—Reuben, Simeon, Levi, Judah, Issachar, Zebulun
- Zilpah—Gad, Asher
- Bilhah—Dan, Naphtali
- Rachel—Joseph

After Leah's sixth son, we have the merest mention of the next child born into the family: a slip of a girl named Dinah. Her brothers will love her and defend her in the worst moment of her life, but then we will never hear of her again.

Jacob worked hard, and under his direction, Laban's herds flourished. When Jacob's first son with Rachel was born, Jacob decided it was time to return to his homeland. Maybe eleven boys was the magic number, or maybe he longed for home, for his parents, and to see if his parents still lived. Maybe it was simply time to transition toward independence. With

Rachel's son's birth, any need to stay near her family disappeared; she'd produced a boy, securing her marital status. Otherwise, Jacob could have returned her to Laban and headed off with the rest of his brood, leaving beautiful and loved Rachel behind.

"Send me on my way," he told Laban. After many years of labor, Jacob only wanted out. "Give me my wives and children, for whom I have served you, and I will be on my way. You know how much work I've done for you."

For the first time, we glimpse some level of spirituality in Laban, though he was not looking to the one true God for his insight. "Please stay," Laban said. "I have learned by divination that the Lord has blessed me because of you." Although this wouldn't require divination, just a quick overview of the facts since Jacob arrived. A little counting of sheep. A huge family. A flourishing farm.

"The little you had before I came has increased greatly, and the Lord has blessed you wherever I have been." But now, Jacob said, it's time to take care of my own family. Jacob agreed to stay, with payment in the form of any sheep and goats that were speckled or spotted, and all dark-colored lambs. "My honesty will testify for me in the future," he told Laban.

This remarkable statement gives pause. Previously Jacob was never a person for whom his honesty or integrity would testify. Quite the opposite, in fact. He ran away with his reputation soundly intact: Jacob the liar, the cheat, the heel. But now, he had turned his hand to honest labor and was becoming an honest man.

Jacob was reforming. People can change. This won't be the end of his journey toward integrity, and, as for most everyone, backsliding is likely. But for today, we notice. For our own sakes, and for the sakes of the people we know and love: change is possible. It's never too late to change the way we live, the way we relate to people, the way we work. Today, whether we tend sheep, an office, a home, or an entire school-yard of children — wherever we are, we take heart.

Our past reputation need not own us or determine our actions from this day forward. With God's help and our own good, honest work, change is possible. We, like Jacob, can redefine ourselves. Sometimes, a little (or a lot of) sweat of the brow and hand to the plow is good for what ails us.

TRAVELING MERCY

Dear one,
People can change.
You can change.
Your people can change.
And I'd love to help with that.
Don't give up tomorrow
Because of yesterday,
But decide today
To embrace the new day
With a new start
On your new heart.
It's not too late.
Not too soon.
The time is just right.

NOTE TO SELF

Today is a good day for a new start.

THE GOD WHO SEES . . . AND LEADS

"I have seen all that Laban has been doing to you."

—GENESIS 31:12

Jealousy creates liars of many, and Laban's sons started lies—more deceit!—about Jacob when Jacob prospered. He had worked tirelessly and endured brutal outdoor conditions, but the boss's sons reframed it. "Jacob has taken everything our father owned and has gained all this wealth from what belonged to our father" (Gen. 31:1).

These brothers, who appear from out of nowhere in the last few paragraphs of the story, suddenly grasped for the prosperity they had been too incapable or somehow too unavailable to work for. Their lies worked the expected magic on Laban, whose attitude toward Jacob changed noticeably.

But God noticed too, and told Jacob, "Go back to the land of your fathers and to your relatives, and I will be with you" (Gen. 31:3). God's promise never changed, God hadn't budged. "I will be with you." At just the right time, God again sent word.

As Jacob made plans to leave with his family, in the midst of the conflict with Laban, he recounted a vital dream. An

angel of the Lord appeared to him. "I have seen all that Laban
has been doing to you," God said. For all those lonely years
in the fields, the days and nights of agony, the hard work and
personal losses, God said, "I have seen." God saw Laban steal
all the spotted, speckled, and striped sheep, in direct opposi-
tion to the agreement he had made with Jacob (Gen. 30:34).
God saw. God sees.

All those nights when Jacob took stock of the sheep and
realized he'd again been swindled. Or when the wild animals
stole more of Laban's sheep, which Jacob deducted from his
own herd rather than Laban's.

And for us, God's word is the same. For all those people
who have sorely treated you, "I have seen." I have seen all
the pain. I have seen the tears. I have seen the judgment, the
unfairness. I have seen. I, God, have seen. For all those nights
when you felt alone. I have seen. For all those moments of
lostness, I have seen. For all those wounds. I have seen. For
all the disappointments, I have seen. When others received
the job or the promotion or the favors or the bonuses, I have
seen.

God doesn't leave Jacob hanging there in a field of dreams
with a reassurance that is theoretical but impractical. He
didn't leave Jacob with a nice sermon about God always
being with us, even though life is wretched. Sure, it's true.
You and I know this is true. But sometimes we need more
than theory and the mental certainty of truth. We need a
reminder, and we need direction. God concludes the dream
with, "I am the God of Bethel, where you anointed a pillar
and where you made a vow to me" (Gen. 31:13).

"I am," God said. I am the God of Abraham, the God of Isaac. And I am the God of you, Jacob. The one who met you at Bethel, the God who promised to be with you and to bring you back to your homeland. That God, the one God, the God to whom you vowed (Gen. 28:13–15). God reminded Jacob of his past, of his promises to God, and of God's promises to him.

Then, at last, the directive Jacob had been waiting for: "Now leave this land at once and go back to your native land." "Arise, leave!" The Hebrew reads. Jacob will be given the opportunity to fulfill the vows he made.

Whether we physically leave our current locale, we return to the land of our faith, to our homeland in God's heart. To the truth that the God who promised Jacob is the God who promises us, the God who sees Jacob is the God who sees us. Arise! Leave! We arise from our doubts, we leave our discouragement, we move to the land of faith.

TRAVELING MERCY

Dear one,
I am the God who sees,
The God who knows.
I have seen your pain,
The mistreatment,
The unfairness.
I see.
And I have seen
Your hard work,
Your growth,
Your leaps and bounds
Toward integrity.
I see.
Don't run from me;
I haven't budged,
Haven't changed.
And now it's time
To return to the land of your faith,
To the land of your first love.
Right here,
Right now.

NOTE TO SELF

God sees, so I can breathe.

ANCESTOR WORSHIP

When Laban had gone to shear his sheep, Rachel
stole her father's household gods.

—GENESIS 31:19

Family antiques, with their gleaming glaze and their
gracious curves. I love them. The rounded globe lamps, the
claw-footed chairs, my grandmother's linen chests, and the
Civil War-era sofa. I love them. The matching dressers with their
oversized mirrors on thick arms of curving mahogany. Even
though their history is sketchy (I bought them for seventy-five
dollars at a thrift store), I love them.

They've been family, silent spectators of so much family
story, eyewitnesses of generations of people and their lives.
They've cradled our heads and held our treasures and our
clothes. They've lightened our rooms and provided rest.

As we packed to move, my husband Rich watched the
boxes accumulate. I threw away almost nothing and gave
away a lot with very little of value to me, knowing that the
clock ticked without grace toward a very quick close on our
home. I refused to make decisions in a hurry. "You have to
break your ties with your past, Jane," Rich said. "You have
to let go of some of this furniture."

I dismissed the possibility. Absolutely not. I loved them. They spoke to me of grace where none could be found and bore witness to longevity in a short-lived world. They whispered quality and taste in a cheap cardboard, fiberboard, and plastic industry. They also lured me with safety, because they are truly irreplaceable: We couldn't afford to buy new or even used if we relinquished these keepsakes. Rachel longed to take treasures of the past on her move; I did too. Only I'd find a more honest way to go about keeping them (plus, they were too big for me to hide by sitting on them).

The size of our next home forced us to measure and scheme. I gloated. I knew it! All the furniture would fit. My husband, greatly relieved not to have to battle me over the antiques, relaxed. But we didn't count on all the boxes, hundreds of boxes—our lives contained in cardboard and sealed with many rolls of wrapping tape.

At 4 a.m., while the movers tried to shoehorn the last of our possessions into our small home, and rain poured and thunder cracked overhead, I turned to my husband in our dark and overstuffed house. "I repent."

"Of what?"

"Of everything." Nothing like a vague and meaningless statement.

He raised his eyebrows.

I swept my hands around the room. We had, literally, twelve inches of passage from the foyer through the living room. Some would call it a great room, but its size refuses me the dishonesty. Furniture stacked to the ceiling, at least eighteen straight-backed chairs, and who knows how many end tables and boxed lamps. Even though the boxes of books and my entire office would sooner (or later, it turns out) be moved to its new locale off-site and would eliminate some furniture density, we owned too much.

In the dark, with humidity rising off our overworked bodies and the rain pummeling outside, I finally recognized the truth. This was modern-day ancestor worship. These were my household gods. Not that my forebearers were of Abraham or Isaac or Jacob stature. But their era of life, of hard work and gracious rest, spoke to me, wooed me. Comforted me.

Loving a lifestyle or the genteel appearance of a lifestyle to the extent that today's life is squeezed out of the equation cuts ruts of its own.

Family keepsakes ruled Rachel. So much that she stole them. While I wouldn't do that, what control would these idols, these gods I'd made of my predecessors' possessions, have on my life?

We—OK, I—have more to give away. Much more. My grandparents? They couldn't take their possessions with them, which is how these lovely items ended up in our home. Nor can I take my possessions, or theirs, with me. The sooner we accept that, the lighter the load in this wilderness journey. And en route, I will try to leave behind the doubt that bound me to those pieces. Because just as God provided for Jacob, scheming Jacob, every step of his way through the desert, so will God provide for us.

TRAVELING MERCY

Dear one,
Your stuffed life
Leaves little room
To grow,
To spin,
To twirl in joy,
Let alone rest.
So let some stuff go.
Cut your ties
With your hopes for the past,
For the past is past.
And now we work together
Toward the future.
Together.
I promise.

NOTE TO SELF

Less ownership equals less emotional attachment,
which equals more freedom.

A FAITHFUL WITNESS

"This heap is a witness, and this pillar is a witness."

—GENESIS 31:52

Sometimes a simple miracle sets us on our feet, and for the first time in the records of Rachel and Leah, we see one: the sisters in agreement about leaving Laban and setting off with their shared husband, Jacob. In unison, the sisters raise their chorus: Our father has sold us off, given away our inheritance, and regards us as foreigners, "so do whatever God has told you" (Gen. 31:16).

While Jacob gathered the family, herds, and belongings, and Laban was off giving his sheep a haircut (or rather, the flocks Jacob raised for him), Rachel sneaked into Laban's home and pilfered the household gods. Whether this was for her own security, to give her a taste of home, or to annoy her father, who knows. But was he ever irate when he discovered Jacob's flight and the household gods missing.

Laban chased Jacob and the family, dragging along his relatives for reinforcement, and overtook the refugees in the hill country of Gilead. En route, God spoke to Laban in a dream and warned him to be careful with Jacob.

Laban's fury didn't wane, and when he found Jacob's encampment, he lit into him with all sorts of fairy tales. He would have celebrated them and sent them all off with a feast and music and dancing, so why would Jacob run away, carrying off his daughters "like captives in war"? But his next words are telling, "Why did you steal my gods?" Laban's motives really seem to be about the profit he's losing and those pocket gods.

Jacob's leaf had thoroughly turned over. He answered honestly, "I was afraid, because I thought you would take your daughters away from me by force." And because he didn't know Rachel stole the gods, he gave Laban full permission to search the tents. When Laban came to Rachel's tent, there she sat on the camel basket, in the tent, with the household gods underneath. What a statement about the value of those little statues.

Jacob lashed into Laban for his manhunt, and was so convincing about all that he had given to Laban that the older man relented. "Come now, let's make a covenant, you and I, and let it serve as a witness between us" (Gen. 31:44).

After he found a large stone and set it in place as a pillar, Jacob gathered the family. Laban issued a witness of sorts: "May the LORD keep watch between you and me when we are away from each other. If you mistreat my daughters or if you take any wives besides my daughters . . . remember that God is a witness between you and me" (see Gen. 31:49–50).

The watchtower, the witness heap. In that comfort, we can all abide; God is a witness between us, God sees, and under God's loving and watchful eye, we can learn to honor one another.

Perhaps, like Jacob and Laban and all their families, we could follow their next lead: prepare a feast and eat. Together.

A sign of unity. Of family. The family of Abraham, of Isaac, of Jacob, and of the Christ.

TRAVELING MERCY

Dear one,
I am your rock,
But I'm not a stone,
A pocket god
Or a household charm.
I'm issuing fair warning:
I'm watching over you,
A faithful witness,
And will guard you
And protect you in all
Your ways.
So relax your guard
With one another
And prepare a feast,
And learn what
Family is.
A union.
You, me, we.

NOTE TO SELF

Unity is a miracle. Seek it, today.

THE ONLY PRAYER

"O God of my father Abraham, God of my father Isaac,
Lord, you who said to me, 'Go back.'"

—Genesis 32:9

Jacob left the time with Laban and the witness stone and headed next toward a potentially deadly reunion with his brother. He met, again, the band of angels. Only for Jacob is this rare term for this group of angels used in Scripture: the first time on Jacob's flight away from home toward Harran in the place he named Bethel, house of God (Gen. 28:12) and now, many years later, on his return. The story swings full circle, bookending Jacob's travels with the same troop of angels. Their presence confirmed for him his calling by God. God had him covered.

For the first time in his recorded history, we hear Jacob pray. He didn't pray at other key moments that we know of—not when he'd wronged his brother Esau or his father, not even when God appeared to him in the field while Jacob slept on a stone. His father, Isaac, begged God to intervene and bring a child when Rebekah proved infertile, but no prayers from Jacob are recorded throughout Rachel's despair and struggle.

But now, finally, perhaps he realized everything was at stake. Perhaps he at last recognized that his life at no time was solely about him, but always about his life in community with the people God had blessed him with. His sense of responsibility had begun to show and his gratitude. He had done more than survive; he had grown in those years—through hardship, loss, contention in the home, and a conniving and abusive father-in-law.

Jacob resolved that conflict with Laban peaceably, and then headed forward. He knew that the worst may yet be in front of him: his confrontation with Esau. His past rushed at his present. He truly expected to come out of that meeting much worse for wear (if even alive at all). He trembled with terror for himself and also for his family.

And then, *then* the angels greeted him, the angels whose very presence reminded him of God's promise long ago, a lifetime ago, a different person ago. So Jacob prayed. He identified God by God's promises, made before Jacob left Harran for good: "O God of my father Abraham . . . you who said to me, 'Go back to your country and your relatives, and I will make you prosper'" (Gen. 32:9). And God loves to keep those promises. God loves to fulfill those promissory notes, and I imagine is delighted that we remember, that we trust him enough to bring it up, and that we look for that fulfillment from his hand.

And then, Jacob the proud actually confessed, "I am unworthy of all the kindness and faithfulness you have shown your servant" (Gen. 32:10). This is enormous, for a man who stole the most significant gifts possible as a younger man.

For what is theft, other than a statement that we can take what is not ours, by whatever means we choose, that we deserve what another has a right to because we have more value? Jacob, this reformed thief, humbled himself and acknowledged his complete unworthiness.

Then, hear Jacob's heart-cry: "Save me, I pray." Save me from the hand of my brother, save me from the deserved results of my past crimes, save my children and their mothers. Do what you do, God. Save.

Jacob closed his prayer with what he knew to be true: God's word. He again reminded God of the promise of descendants like the sand of the sea, too many to be counted.

Here are we, knowing we deserve none of God's faithfulness and kindness, knowing that we, too, have thieved our way to the present, knowing that without God's provision—for however good we have been, we are never good enough to be in God's presence, never good enough to deserve God's forgiveness—our past will catch up to us and destroy us and those we love. Without God we bring our house down around our own heads, and without God we collapse under the debris of our lives.

And we, like Jacob, trembling with fear, plead the only prayer we know. "Save me, I pray."

TRAVELING MERCY
Dear one,
It's the only prayer you need:
"Save me."
Always feel free to remind me
Of my promises to you.
Although I will not forget,
This helps you to remember
I am faithful
And I keep my word.

NOTE TO SELF
Remind, confess, ask.
It's all I need to remember.

THE OLD IS GONE

"What is your name?"

—Genesis 32:27

Until Jacob reached Harran, he lived headlong into the meaning of his name: "deceiver," "supplanter," "heel grasper." He looked out for number one, himself, showing no regard or compassion for anyone in his family. The type of appetite he expressed was differed from Esau's, but otherwise, both were consumed by an appetite for themselves.

But after his exile, Jacob's dream on the stone marked a turning point in his life. Once he reached Harran, we begin to see a hardworking, loyal man, honest in his toil in the fields. He worked as a hired hand rather than as a son for Laban, and bore the loss of sheep himself. With the flocks, Jacob spent brutal nights and days in the cold and the heat, the rain and the misery. He brought nothing but his staff with him on this journey, for he had not yet come into the inheritance he had stolen. Yet he left rich in herds and servants and with a family line nearly established.

On this side of the rock, he had behaved, largely, with integrity, this man who once lived with deceit. He was becoming himself, his best self. For Jacob, well over ninety years of age, it was not too late.

As he headed for his homeland, back to his family, one more encounter set the stage for the rest of his life. He readied to meet his brother, certain that Esau would be filled with hatred and still murderous. Jacob's fear does him credit as he faced the outcome of his own actions. Just like Esau as the firstborn, he had scraped together a living when he could have lived off his family's goodness.

In this attitude of humility and fear, he strategized a plan of peace offerings for his brother. He moved his family and all his possessions across the Jabbok River, then returned to the north side of the river. Jacob, alone, struggled with an unknown man and refused to be wrestled down: "When the man saw that he could not overpower him, he touched the socket of Jacob's hip so that his hip was wrenched. Then the man said, 'Let me go, for it is daybreak'" (Gen. 32:25–26).

All of Jacob's life, his decisions, his movement toward wholeness, rushed toward this moment of encounter. He had fought his way, against his own character and against that of others in his life. He had worked hard with increasing integrity. And now, as he returned to perhaps the most difficult relationship he'd left behind, he refused to be unchanged.

"I will not let you go unless you bless me," Jacob told the man.

Mark this milestone moment, this moment of change. The man asked, "What is your name?"

"Jacob." Jacob owned his name, his identity, and all that his name meant. Surely, as he spoke, his whole life skidded past his eyes—his trickery, his lies, his selfishness, his running, his shame.

"Your name will no longer be Jacob, but Israel, because you have struggled with God and with humans, and have overcome." In humility and reverence, Jacob named the place *Peniel*, "face of God." "Because I saw God face to face, and yet my life was spared" (Gen. 32:30).

Perhaps this is, ultimately, the source of our fascination with Jacob: the story of a man who succumbed to his base nature and lived down to his name, but whose longing for the deep things of God would not allow him to rest there. His journey is our journey, a journey of seeking, of intervention, of mistakes and love and hardship.

You are no longer Jacob. You are no longer who you once were. And we, who have named Christ as our Messiah, hear these words with New Testament ears. We are no longer dead in our trespasses and sins. We are new creations, new in Christ. The old has passed away, the new has come.

Though we walk with a limp, we walk forward into a new day, each dawn a new chance at life. A day to face our fears, to greet our enemies with peace offerings, to respect and love those we encounter.

We are no longer Jacob. We are no longer who we once were.

TRAVELING MERCY

Dear one,
You are no longer Jacob.
I am dancing with joy.
You are new.
A new creation.
New in Christ.
You may limp
But you are no longer
Who you once were.
So face down your fear.
Walk forward
Into this new day.

NOTE TO SELF

Today, new day, new me.

NAME POWER

"Your name will no longer be Jacob."

—GENESIS 32:28

On the stage, what's in a name may mean the difference between obscurity and fame. Thus, Nicolas Kim Coppola became Nicolas Cage; Dana Elaine Owens turned into Queen Latifah; Benjamin Géza Affleck-Boldt became Ben Affleck; and Eleanor Nancy Gow became Elle Macpherson. After her agent dreamed about unlocking a briefcase, Alicia Augello Cook became Alicia Keys. Judy Garland, the beloved lead in *The Wizard of Oz*, changed her name from Frances Ethel Gumm. Helen Mirren was once Ilyena Vasilievna Mironov, and Natalie Wood started life as Natalia Nikolaevna Zacharenko. We know Marion Robert Morrison better as John Wayne.

The performers wanted to live into their gifts. Who can blame them for seeking an edge by creating a new name? Whether we change our birth certificate or not, we don't have to be saddled with a name that offers us nothing to live into.

Surely God wants us to grow up into the image he sees for us, the people he created us to be. Who is that person? Perhaps that is the best question we can seek to answer: How does

God see me? What gifts have I received? What character traits could I improve upon? Where is there growing room?

After the second deception, Esau said, "Not for nothing was he named Jacob, the Heel. Twice now he's tricked me: first he took my birthright and now he's taken my blessing" (Gen. 27:36 MSG). Jacob who deceived, who lived a lifestyle of stealing. Jacob who lived down to his name. Jacob had room to grow. God didn't abandon him there in that field, in the dark of his confusion, in the regret that trailed behind him. Rather, God came to him and called him forward.

If you could name yourself for a prevalent trait, what would it be? Happy? Miserable? Patient? Angry? Answer honestly, with a careful self-inventory, not with the "I'm a Christian so I shouldn't think highly of myself" or with the "I follow God so I must pretend to display all the fruit of the spirit all the time" attitude.

Then there are the names that others press upon us, whether by their words or their actions. Names such as Forlorn, Unloved, Untalented, Stupid, Lame, Ugly, Failure, Spineless.

We do not have to live down to those names, to live under their oppression. But a good transition from old to new requires work, especially considering what those names often cost us. How have they hindered you or forced you to assume a guise different from who you really are? In what ways did they inhibit you from recognizing your gifts and talents? From loving honestly?

Then, begin to ask, "How does God see me? What does God say about me?" Just as with Jacob, God meets us all in our despair and changes our names. Jacob became Israel, One

Who Wrestles with God. He dared to say to God, "I refuse to let go until you bless me." And God blessed him, and changed his name. From Jacob the Heel to Israel the God-Wrestler.

God sees your potential, sees who you really are. What will you be called?

TRAVELING MERCY

Dear one,
Remember those old names?
Count their costs
To your soul,
And then, refocus.
When will you see yourself
As I see you?
Soon I hope.
Here are some of my names for you:
Beloved,
Precious,
Delighted in,
Graced,
Gift,
Worthy,
Beloved.
Oh, I said that already.

NOTE TO SELF

What does God call me?

A GOOD NAME

A good name is more desirable than great riches;
to be esteemed is better than silver or gold.

—PROVERBS 22:1

Some children get the super cute names, the top of the chart names, movie star names without ever having to change them. Others get names that feel like a curse, a playground joke. Once I knew someone named Candy Cain. Then there's a woman named Michelle who married a man named Michael Michelle, so her name ended up like a stutter (or a song title or a rock star), Michelle Michelle.

Maybe they love their names. I hope so. But maybe you don't love yours. What does your name mean, and to what might it be calling you? Sometimes people name their children as an act of prophecy, calling them up to their potential or describing their character. If your name, like Jacob's, has negative meanings, invite God to call you by a new name.

My name plagued me when I considered it, which wasn't all that frequently since I wasn't a particularly introspective child. Jane rhymes with nothing very good—Plain Jane, to name a happy common couplet children loved to use on the swing sets or bus. Although they could have been using the homonym Plane Jane, since I was all angles and sharp edges and flat sides. Either way, I never knew the real meaning of my name, and I knew only one other person with that name. Jane hasn't topped any most popular name list ever, as far as I can tell.

So when I learned that my name means "grace," it hushed my dissonance. Grace? Grace. I breathe that in. Jane means "God is gracious," the name books tell me. That I want to explore. But it also means, I hesitate to add, "God's gracious gift."

Hesitate, because I am so often far from gracious and far from a gift to anyone. When someone gave me a name mug with that inscription, my embarrassment and shame peaked. I hid the cup and never told anyone about my name's meaning. I am well aware of my own hypocrisy and don't need anyone else to call me on it, nor a cup reminding me what a mess I can be.

At some breakthrough (or breaking point), I brought it out in the open, determined to live my life by living my name. Then after an ugly day (or maybe week or month) of living far from whom God intended me to become, far from a gift, far from gracious, I pitched the cup into a giveaway box.

Someone told me, at a retreat in Pennsylvania that my middle name, Ann, also means "God is gracious" or "God's gracious gift." So my name, really, is Grace Grace. Double Grace, a doubling of God's graciousness.

Home again, on a deep breath, I found the giveaway box and dug out the cup. God is relentless about inviting us forward. Me, you, Jacob the deceiver. All of us, wanderers, seeking some portal toward heaven, some experience of God's providing hope to move us ahead.

So pull out your cup, invite God to clarify your name, and begin to drink and live deeply.

TRAVELING MERCY

Dear one,
Others' names for you pain me
And pain you.
But
You are far from plain
In my sight.
I am plain crazy
About you.
So turn your face toward me
And look me in the eyes
And hear this,
My gift to you:
I love you.
Will that
Do?

NOTE TO SELF

Regardless of others' names for me,
God calls me Beloved.

RUNNING FORWARD

Jacob looked up and there was Esau.

—GENESIS 33:1

Though he's never far from our mind, the next time we see Esau, Jacob is hauling back from laboring under Laban, that duplicitous uncle, his mother's brother. During Jacob's years of working like a slave there, God blessed him abundantly. He earned, literally from his work, two wives, Rachel and Leah. Their two maids added children to the family, and they all had begun the process of building a nation.

But escaping Laban's trickery became paramount to that construction. Jacob rounded up his extensive family, animals, and other belongings. Home called, and off they trundled. En route, God wrestled with Jacob in the night, and Jacob, strong Jacob, refused to let go until God blessed him.

The only issue, of course, was his maligned brother, Esau. At their last encounter, Esau swore vengeance against Jacob. Surely in Esau's eyes, Jacob the deceiver, the cheat, the heel lived on. Jacob's return home meant returning to the man who wanted to kill him. His picture wallpapered the post office of Esau's heart and topped the most-wanted-criminal list.

Jacob tried everything in his power to secure safe reentry: He packed up loads of animals and sent them ahead as gifts. He packed up his family and sent them ahead of him. (This seems less than courageous, but he must have had some plan to disarm Esau with all the women and children.)

Jacob crawled forward in great fear and distress, and we see for the first time the impact of his thievery. His fearful return indicates his lack of wisdom in the way he left—had he left cleanly, he could have returned at peace. Hopefully, his fear also shows remorse over the birthright and the blessing.

Here's the beauty. Jacob, limping from his encounter with God, trembling with anxiety, searched the horizons for signs of his brother and a marauding band of vengeance-minded troops until he at last saw Esau headed toward him. Jacob's heart smacked his rib cage for escape. Four hundred men flanked Esau. Jacob likely remembered the stories of Abraham, who with 318 men took down an entire roster of kings. But wait. Esau's bow wasn't drawn and no knife flashed between his teeth.

In fact, Esau rushed to Jacob like he was a rock star, a long lost loved one. The years of separation had worked a miracle on Esau. He chose to release his anger and bitterness and refused to allow his heart to harden like a red brick baked in the desert sun. He'd put his past behind him, where it could no longer trip him up. Esau saw his brother and "ran to meet Jacob and embraced him; he threw his arms around his neck and kissed him. And they wept" (Gen. 33:4). They wept. Two grown men, long grown apart, separated by ages-old enmity and lust and theft and revenge.

The joy of reunion radiated from Jacob. His words move me. "To see your face is like seeing the face of God" (Gen. 33:10). The wall of fear and hatred dissolved in the warmth of Esau's welcome. Esau's strong arms circled Jacob and taught the deceiver the most valuable blessing of all: forgiveness. And Esau demonstrated at last the fulfillment of his father's blessing, "You will throw his yoke from off your neck" (Gen. 27:40). Esau, no longer yoked to resentment and hatred. And Jacob, free at last from his past.

Now he could truly believe, and live into, and move forward with, his new name: Israel. God fought for him.

TRAVELING MERCY
Dear one,
Don't be yoked by anger
Or bitterness.
Don't allow hatred
To chain you.
Throw off that yoke.
And about your past:
Figure out where you
Can apologize.
Do it quickly.
Ask for forgiveness
And walk forward
Into relationship,
Into life.
I am fighting
For you.

NOTE TO SELF
What is my yoke? I want to walk free.

A COVENANT RENEWAL

*The terror of God fell on the towns all around
them so that no one pursued them.*

—Genesis 35:5

Esau hugged Jacob's neck and they parted ways, Jacob promising to follow him home at a slower pace. Instead, Jacob routed his family to Shechem. Whether he intentionally lied to his brother after such a warm reunion, or just considered the destination and the shift in plans irrelevant, that change would result in unspeakable tragedy and bloodshed for his family. He bought a little plot of land outside the city, the only ground we know that Jacob owned. There the local prince raped Dinah, and her brothers took bloody vengeance. (See Gen. 34 for the full the story.) Jacob must have regretted his detour for the rest of his days.

In the midst of this pain, surely one of Jacob's worst and most heartbreaking seasons to date, he again heard from God: "Go up to Bethel and settle there, and build an altar there to God, who appeared to you when you were fleeing from your brother Esau" (Gen. 35:1).

Imagine Jacob's relief, in the wake of his family's trauma—which would have made anyone wonder where God was, exactly—to hear again from his God. And his heart perked up with certainty, as well: We are starting over. We will live our lives toward God from now on. He gathered his household and all his people and announced this new direction. "Get rid of all your foreign gods! Purify yourselves! Change your clothes! We are going to meet with God, the God who has been with me everywhere I've gone," he instructed, "The God," he continued, "who answered me in the day of my distress" (Gen. 35:2–3).

So stricken were they all, perhaps still reeling from their family tragedy, they emptied their pockets of their lucky charms, jewelry, and statues, then gathered the household gods, both stolen and long in their families. In a sweeping statement of solidarity they moved as one toward Bethel and toward a relationship with this God, Jacob's God, the God of Abraham and Isaac, and now, their God.

Under the oak at Shechem, the scene of the tragedy, Jacob buried the idols, and he and his loved ones and all their people set out for Bethel.

Jacob was learning what we, too, sometimes have difficulty living out: that God doesn't fit in pockets, that God is not a good-luck charm, a rabbit foot to stroke in times of distress. This God, the God of the highest heaven, the God who appears in dreams, who makes enormous promises and then delivers on them, this God will not be contained by the entire earth, let alone a stone statue we place on our mantels.

Something holy happened, there at the scene of their family's devastation and the moment of their great turnaround. Something so deep and profound, so sacred, that as they buried the idols and moved as one toward Bethel, "the terror of God fell on the towns all around them so that no one pursued them" (Gen. 35:5).

At Bethel, the site of God's revelation, God appeared again. The place of intersection between heaven and earth, this place where the band of angels had greeted Jacob years before, became once again the site of God's appearance.

God said to him, "Your name is Jacob, but you will no longer be called Jacob; your name will be Israel" (Gen. 35:10). Always, God wants us to remember who we truly are, who we are called to be. To remember our name, to know that God is our God and the one who directs our paths. To live under our name, child of God.

But God wasn't finished. Jacob's journey, like ours, was far from over, and he would need yet another reminder. "I am God Almighty." *El Shaddai*, the sovereign King of the world, the God who grants, who blesses, who judges. The sovereign God, the mighty God, spoke into Jacob's soul, and wonder filled him. And joy, such joy. That mighty God would speak into his life and would watch over him wherever he traveled.

And then, the enormous promise, expanded from his grandfather Abraham and his father Isaac, "Be fruitful and increase in number. A nation and a community of nations will come from you, and kings will be among your descendants. The land I gave to Abraham and Isaac I also give to you, and I will give this land to your descendants after you" (Gen. 35:11–12).

At that holy place, the place of God's appearance, Bethel, Jacob again set a stone pillar, poured out a drink offering on it, and anointed it with oil. This would be the reminder, for him, and for all who passed by for generations, that God Almighty is God Faithful, God Present, and God Sees.

TRAVELING MERCY

Dear one,
I Am.
I am God Almighty,
God who is present,
God who accompanies you,
God who carries you,
God who cares.
Your journey is long,
The road steep,
But I am faithful.
And you will see
There are tears to come
And trials.
Your moments of heartbreak
Far from over.
But the joy,
The wonder,
We will face it all
Together
And overcome.

NOTE TO SELF

Me plus God equals hope.

DESERT GRIEF

As [Rachel] breathed her last—for she was dying—
she named her son Ben-Oni.

—Genesis 35:18

Before Jacob and company arrived home in Mamre, Rachel, at last pregnant with another child, went into labor. As the baby was born, Rachel's life slipped away.[1] She named her son, "son of my trouble," Ben-Oni. And Jacob, grieving his wife but loving his son, changed the boy's name to Benjamin, "son of my right hand." What anguish, losing his beloved wife before reaching home. A painful flashback to Genesis 30:1, Rachel begging of Jacob, "Give me children or I'll die." Her final child was the death of her.

So much grief. Sarah, dying of heartbreak.[2] Rebekah, never seeing her son again. Rachel, struggling with her infertility. Leah, the unloved one, grieving for her daughter. So much grief on this journey, then and now. Whether we grieve another's death, or other losses, the lifelong companion of grief refuses to be ignored.

At a recent dinner event, my new friend Lynnea buried her hands in her lap beneath the tablecloth. Beautifully coifed and dressed, she looked as lifeless as a cardboard cutout.

When I asked about her week, she shared the most recent installment of her desert chronicle.

She'd already been journeying through the wilderness for a long time. After her mother's initial diagnosis of Alzheimer's some years ago, the disease stalled, allowing her mother to live independently for quite a while. But last year, after an accident, her mother's body downward-spiraled in protest. Complications during recovery short-circuited her system. Body processes slowed and her memory declined at a steep pitch. She could no longer be left alone, and yet enough of her mind remained for her to refuse twenty-four-hour care. So Lynnea and her sister took turns tending to her. On top of their day jobs and family commitments, on top of church responsibilities and the need and longing to meet with God, and on top of near-desperate exhaustion.

Now we sat at my table, after eight years of Lynnea caring for her mother and watching her deteriorate. Those years of erosion from gradual, unending grief, and the weight of care, bowed Lynnea's spirit. Her mother died two months ago, which devastated Lynnea. Then came house cleaning and refurbishing. Every day, another task completed. Every day, one day closer to pounding the For Sale sign in the yard. It felt like a stake driven into her heart. This past week, they finished painting and neighbors stopped by to compliment the color choices. It was a type of good-bye from the neighbors of so many years to the woman who had lived there so valiantly. The finality of that last good-bye nearly dismantled Lynnea.

Grief is a whole-body response. Her boss, knowing this, pulled her aside. "Lynnea, I'm worried about you. We have free counseling services. Please take care of yourself. We need you."

Over dinner together, we spoke of finding places for grieving and of deliberately taking time away from her crushing commitments to process the journey and begin to heal.

In a nation and culture where we can hire out just about every task, no one else can do our healing work. Experts or friends can help us move toward healing. But they can't heal us, and they can't do the work necessary for us to heal. We can't expect others to have the magic ticket. Healing is a commitment we make, ourselves. We may not have many choices in the itinerary. But the choice to heal is ours, and it is essential.

Lynnea considers herself one of the fortunates. She recognized her grief and pain, and chose, for her own sake and for the people around her, to seek help. But so often, we don't even know we have inner work to do.

Finding our new name takes a lifetime, and moving toward a new name requires this move toward healing. Wilderness living may highlight our worst, so that we can drag that jumbled mess of emotions and hopes and disappointments and sorrows to God. So that we can make a deliberate decision that the wilds will not win over us, but that instead we will wrest from them whatever good God has in store. And then, no matter how long or short, how solved or unsolved our travel problems, we won't waste the wilderness. And the wilderness won't waste us.

TRAVELING MERCY

Dear one,
The wastelands won't waste you
Nor will your grief and sorrow.
Your sadness will last for the moment
But take heart.
I am the God of the desert
And am waiting for your cry.
Turn to me.
Let me help.
Hide your face in my shoulder.
Cry out your tears.
And let's find that healing place
Together.
Joy will come
In the mourning.
And in the morning.

NOTE TO SELF

I will wrest the good from the wilderness,

though it means mourning.

NOTES

1. After Laban's idols disappeared and Laban chased Jacob et al., Jacob vowed to Laban that if the idols were found in their possession, the thief would be put to death. Some Jews believe that Rachel's death is the fulfillment of that vow.

2. Jewish tradition believes that Sarah died of heartbreak when she realized Abraham intended to sacrifice Isaac on the altar. This is why they consider Isaac to be thirty-seven-years old when he walked to the altar with his father. Sarah died at 127, and gave birth to Isaac at ninety.

A BLESSING OF PARTING

To him who is able to do immeasurably more
than all we ask or imagine.

—EPHESIANS 3:20

So many years ago, Laban and his mother huddled around Rebekah before she left Harran to marry Isaac. With financial matters settled and the camels saddled, only the good-byes remained. Laban wasn't stingy with the blessing. Even he would have been surprised, however, to learn how God honored his traditional prayer over Rebekah, his only sister: "May you increase to thousands upon thousands; may your offspring possess the cities of their enemies" (Gen. 24:60).

To increase to thousands upon thousands was enormous thinking, exponential given the small clusters of people groups in and around Harran. Pretty optimistic praying, considering that, so far, the family under the mantel of blessing consisted of Abraham, Sarah, and Isaac. At the time of the prayer, Rebekah was marrying into an upstart family, a tiny family with a great big promise. Though her grandfather Terah might have opted out of the family tour of Canaan back when God called Abraham and said, "I will bless you, and make you a blessing, and make you into a large nation," even if the blessing skipped Rebekah's brother personally, it would still impact him and continue down through his family in mind-boggling ways. A large nation, a great nation? This barely begins to describe the future.

Laban, though he couldn't know it, prayed right into God's plans.

That's just one of the things I love about God's economy. God has these gargantuan plans and then invites us to pray, and somehow he weaves us into the giant, eye-popping answer.

Many years later, in a mixture of distress and relief, Rebekah would wave off her favorite son, Jacob, who would arrive winded from his long jaunt from Canaan, right at Laban's doorstep. In our wildest imaginings, we don't come up with Jacob marrying not just one, but two of Uncle Laban's daughters. We would never dream of the sheep stealing and conflict, nor the competition between all the women. Even a good novelist wouldn't dare to include the surrogate wives and all those children, all from the same man, the son of Laban's sister Rebekah. But truth, of course, is stranger than fiction.

Thousands upon thousands. Within a few hundred years, even that number would seem small, when the family of Israel escaped from Egypt with 1.5 million men, not counting all the wives and children, and returned to the Promised Land. Even Laban, with his secular blessing over his sister Rebekah, would never have dreamed of such a flashy answer.

Nor would we, a thousand-plus years later, imagine that from Jacob's family line, with Leah the unloved wife as the mother, would come the great fulfillment of that blessing: the Christ would be born, who would indeed possess one day the cities of all the enemies. He would conquer not only sin, but also the great enemy, death, and the entire world would be his footstool.

Laban might never have dreamed this, but we know it to be fact. So today, we survey our own lives, all the ridiculous impossibilities and all the places we have stopped dreaming and stopped trusting. We look at the unknowns, the far-fetched hopes. We consider the Jacobs and Esaus in our lives, the Rachels and Leahs. The stolen sheep and the stolen blessings.

And we say, with all those who have gone before us, that truly nothing is impossible with God. Thousands upon thousands?

We are just getting started.

TRAVELING MERCY

Dear one,
I cannot contain
My smile.
Everything in your life
Leads you to today
And I have enormous,
Exciting
Plans for you—
Plans that will surge
Through generations of people
Because you love me
And I love you
And together
We will change
The population of heaven.
Eye has not seen,
Ear has not heard,
You cannot conceive
All that I have prepared for you.
We are just getting started.
I can't wait.

NOTE TO SELF

Thousands upon thousands? Let's get going!

FAMILY REUNION

Jacob came home to his father Isaac in Mamre . . . where Abraham and Isaac had stayed. Isaac lived a hundred and eighty years.

—GENESIS 35:27–28

Homecomings are often bittersweet. People and situations have changed. Life has changed. And for Jacob, after many years home had changed. His mother, who vowed to send for him as soon as Esau's anger dissipated, never sent word and is never mentioned after Jacob left for Harran. Perhaps she died of a broken heart, her marriage no longer stable, her favorite son gone, and Esau bitter. But whatever happened, she did not stand at the gate on tiptoe watching Jacob's return with his flourishing family.

And Isaac, who thought he might be dying decades ago, yet lived! Imagine his disbelief as he heard the word carried through the hills, "Jacob is coming! Your son Jacob returns!" The joy must have filled his lonely soul until he propelled himself up and out to greet his heir, the spiritual head of the family, the one through whom God's blessing and promise would continue.

Oh, the joy, the joy! Twelve grandsons, one yet so young. Imagine, twelve! More than he could have imagined in his wildest, most hopeful dreams. Rambunctious boys, enough to build a nation. The makings of greatness.

He could scarcely contain himself as his trembling hands made careful study of his son, his long gone son. Feeling his face, his beard, his hair, his hands that once deceived him but now, so hardworking and calloused—strong hands, hands that build. Oh, the joy. And Leah, Leah, Jacob's wife, how they would bond. What joy to have her as part of his family. He mourned, never to meet Rachel, the love of his son's life. But those boys! And Dinah, poor wounded girl. Well, Isaac certainly knew something about wounds, and he just might be able to help her heal.

Stories unfolded, of sheep and goats and maids-in-waiting, of Laban and trickery and the amazing thriving of Jacob's flock, of bands of angels and dreams on stone pillows, of desert chases and piles of stones as witnesses, of idols buried and towns in awe of this tribe of people who follow after the mighty God. Isaac sat back, content, filled, free at last, at peace at last.

The birthright had gone to the right son. This man before him lay a moral and spiritual foundation for his family and for the generations of people who would follow. Isaac remembered God's assurance and promise, one of the few times he heard so clearly from God, "Do not be afraid, for I am with you; I will bless you and will increase the number of your descendants for the sake of my servant Abraham" (Gen. 26:24).

Truly, he thought, God had been with him. He needed never fear, not for all these years. Before him, gathered about his knees, sat the loud, living, testosterone-full proofs.

Isaac would live long enough for most of those grandsons to have their own grandsons. He would live, truly live. His mind returned, as it did sometimes, to that time on the altar, to that fateful trip to Moriah with his own father, Abraham. He breathed deeply, secure in God's covering and protection, confident that the God who provides would continue to provide.

And he breathed again, not his last, but his next, and freest, breath ever.

TRAVELING MERCY

Dear one,
It is true
I know the end
From the beginning
And you will be glad
You held on.
The truth is still the truth,
Then and now.
Do not be afraid
For I am with you,
And I will bless you.
And generations of people
Will follow you
Who love me
Because of you
And because I love you.
Everlasting love.

NOTE TO SELF

No fear, God is here.

A REAL CLOSER

Then he breathed his last and died and was gathered to his people.

—Genesis 35:29

I lean back in my chair, feeling as though I've just read the most satisfying novel. Here's the quick storyboard version of the real-life story. Isaac, long-promised child, grows up and nearly gets sacrificed on an altar. God saves him; he marries; and his infertile wife at last conceives twins. The boys, Jacob and Esau, fight even in the womb, and not much changes between them for a long time. They grow up fast, and right after Esau sells his birthright for a bowl of stew, a famine arises in the land. After God convinces Isaac not to flee to Egypt like his father did, the famine evidently resolves because the family history continues and Isaac's crops grow and his flocks, too. Since famines often or even usually result from drought, no wonder the local herders get into fisticuffs with Isaac about the wells and duke it out about water rights.

All of these worries center on food and water. Around survival. Or rather, fear of not surviving.

No wonder Maslow (who's first name, interestingly, was Abraham) placed physiological needs as the base of the heirarchy of needs pyramid. Without food and water, people die, and the process leading to perishing this way is terrifying and painful.

With all those issues resolved, the storyline turns to procreation. Esau decides time's a wastin' and marries two Hittite women who "were a source of grief to Isaac and Rebekah." Why Judith and Basemath create such difficulty, we have no idea, but Esau's parents are desperate enough now to make plans. Isaac is so old that he figures it's time to divvy up his belongings and readies himself to bestow the blessing on his firstborn son.

That goes awry: Jacob receives the blessing through no fault of Esau's but many thanks to Rebekah, and Esau vows to kill his conniving twin. Jacob escapes his threatening brother and flees to Harran to his mother's brother, Laban. There Jacob works for seven years, gets duped into marrying the wrong woman, and then works for years to keep the right woman. In all, they all have a dozen kids, and life gets so crowded and Laban so greedy that Jacob and his tribe head back to the family ranch.

But his beloved Rachel, the woman who stole his heart, dies in childbirth before they arrive home and is buried. This final child, Benjamin, makes the twelfth son for Jacob, and the boys together start a strong foundation for a nation.

Funny enough, Isaac, who had felt old enough to die years before, lives a long time after blessing the wrong boy (or the right boy, depending on your vantage point), sixty more years, in fact. Now, well past ninety himself, Jacob returned from Harran in time to patch up life with Esau and to see his father.

The last word we have about Isaac is, "Isaac lived a hundred and eighty years. Then he breathed his last and died and was gathered to his people, old and full of years. And his sons Esau and Jacob buried him" (see Gen. 35:27–29).

Isaac's life, Jacob's life, my life, your life: full of life, full of surprises, full of mistakes and questions and worries about life and death. Full. Isaac, a hundred and eighty. Old and full of years. Only a few people in the Scriptures receive that description: Abraham, Isaac, David, Jehoiada, and Job. Five people who lived life to the fullest, refusing to simply age but rather, to live clear to their last breath.

Even with all the plot turns. Even with all the trickery. The births, the deaths, the duels, the dreams. The great inheritance of these people turned out to be, not their accumulations or their accomplishments, but their faithful following God and living deeply, living well.

Old and full of years. It sounds like a good epitaph.

TRAVELING MERCY

Dear one,
Life is hard
And then you die,
So people say.
But I say,
Life is hard
And life is good
And I am good
And I am God
No matter what happens.
So live.
Live today.
Live deeply.
Live well.
Live life to the full.
And don't forget to breathe
Along the way
To your last breath.

NOTE TO SELF

Full. Live full.

THE SOLDERED CHAIN

"I am the God of your fathers,
the God of Abraham, Isaac, and Jacob."

—ACTS 7:32

After his twins grow up, Isaac is mentioned seventeen times in the triplet of "Abraham, Isaac, and Jacob"—a chain of three men, broken and mended, soldered together with the fire of God's presence and provision. Three men, covered with the covenant of God's promise, blessed to be a blessing—each critical to the passing along of God's work and will in this world. Their names would be synonymous with God's faithfulness.

We see them, like father, like son; see their resemblances and their differences. We see how they diverted from the path and witness how they sinned. But they are still a triplet, a heritage, father-son-grandson, in spite of all their carryings-on. Their context helped determine both their resistance and their resilience, their balance sheet of character defects and character assets.

So it is with all of us, each critical in the lineage of God's people, each vital to continuing God's work in this world. Each of us, with a background and past essential to becoming who God longs for us to be, the pump of our lives primed to be a blessing in this world. We wouldn't be the same people without our pasts, however hard they might have been, however many people attempted to sacrifice us on altars of expediency or neglect or misshapen priorities or brokenness. And surely there are adults today whose parents sacrificed them on the altar of religion, of legalism, of spiritual fervor. This is not to say that Abraham's leading Isaac to the altar for sacrifice was any of those, but rather that on some level, we can relate to Isaac, though likely on a (hopefully) less traumatic level.

Our past continues to be a critical shaping tool, one that we learn to honor but also to work with, rather than give in to or run away from. We are people who learn from our past and pass along both the learning and the life God gives us.

Isaac could have quit after his binding near Moriah. He could have blamed his father and withdrawn from the running as the chosen heir. There was, after all, Ishmael as a fall-back, and maybe his daddy loved Ishmael better anyway. Isaac could have turned into his storied uncle Lot, pitching his tent closer and closer to evil until he planted himself in the middle of Sin City.

But regardless of wounds, of flashbacks to that terror-filled time on the altar, Isaac stayed the course. He kept faith in the God of his father, Abraham, and didn't we find him paying attention to God meditating there in the field as the curtains drew closed on another day?

And Jacob, in spite of his deceitful ways, ultimately ran in the path God led him, trying to follow the God of his fathers. Both men moved forward toward their true identities, as people loved and called by God.

And so we, too, choose to show up, daily, knowing that our futures are formed by our past experiences and our present decisions. And, perhaps most of all, by our time in the presence of God. There, in the field or in the living room or in the woods or on the jogging path. The prison cell or the factory line. Meditating. Resting our head by faith on a stone pillow. Tending sheep until our passport to the Promised Land arrives.

Faithful. Showing up, daily, in spite of ourselves, because we know what Abraham, Isaac, and Jacob all knew: a promise is a promise.

TRAVELING MERCY
Dear one,
The best is yet to come,
The story not finished.
Don't give up tomorrow
Because of yesterday.
And don't live yesterday
Instead of today.
But show up today,
And we will walk together
Toward a new
Tomorrow.
A new forever.

NOTE TO SELF
Show up. Join hands. Make plans.

ABOUT THE AUTHOR

Jane Rubietta's hundreds of articles about soul care and restoration have appeared in many periodicals, including *Today's Christian Woman*, *Virtue*, *Marriage Partnership*, *Just Between Us*, *Conversations Journal*, *Decision*, *Christian Reader*, *Indeed*, and *Christianity Today*. Some of her books include: *Finding Life*, *Finding the Messiah*, *Finding Your Promise*, *Quiet Places*, *Come Closer*, and *Grace Points*.

She is a dynamic, vulnerable, humorous speaker at conferences, retreats, and pulpits around the world. Jane particularly loves offering respite and soul care to people in leadership. She has worked with Christian leaders and laity in Japan, Mexico, the Philippines, Guatemala, Europe, the US, and Canada.

Jane's husband, Rich, is a pastor, award-winning music producer, and itinerant worship leader. They have three children and make their home surrounded by slightly overwhelming garden opportunities in the Midwest.

For more information about inviting Jane Rubietta to speak at a conference, retreat, or banquet, please contact her at:

Jane@JaneRubietta.com
www.JaneRubietta.com

Finding Jesus in Every Season

Follow author Jane Rubietta on her daily journey through each season of the year to gain perspective, refresh your soul, and continue the journey. Tracing the lives of some of the Bible's greatest characters, these are transformational devotionals that encourage great depth. Walk through these stories from the Bible and experience life as these great characters did, gaining fresh faith and hope for your journey along the way.

A free group leader's guide is available for each devotional at www.wphresources.com.

Finding Your Promise
(spring)
ISBN: 978-0-89827-896-5
eBook: 978-0-89827-897-2

Finding Your Dream
(fall)
ISBN: 978-0-89827-900-9
eBook: 978-0-89827-901-6

Finding Your Name
(summer)
ISBN: 978-0-89827-898-9
eBook: 978-0-89827-899-6

Finding Your Way
(winter)
ISBN: 978-0-89827-894-1
eBook: 978-0-89827-895-8